*You can be*

# DELIVERED!

for being
a blessing
AB

## Raeni Bankole

# *You can be* DELIVERED!

## Raeni Bankole

*Dewalette Creations*

**You Can Be DELIVERED!**

Copyright © 2014 by Raeni Bankole
Paperback ISBN: 978-0-9886747-7-6

Published by Dewalette Creations
Phone: 630-481-6305
Email: info@dewalette.com; dewalette@gmail.com
Website: www.dewalette.com

Cover Design by GodKulture Creative Agency

Printed in the United States of America

# *Dedication*

To the Mighty Man of War who fought and prevailed two
thousand years ago on the Cross of Calvary.

To the Mighty Warrior who delivers lawful captives
from the dungeons of affliction.

To the Mighty Man in Battle who feeds oppressors with
their own flesh and makes them drunk with their own
blood.

To the Captain of Angelic Host be glory and honor
forever!!!

*Shall the prey be taken from the mighty, Or the captives of the
righteous be delivered? But thus says the Lord: "Even the captives
of the mighty shall be taken away, And the prey of the terrible be
delivered; For I will contend with him who contends with you, And
I will save your children. I will feed those who oppress you with their
own flesh, And they shall be drunk with their own blood as with
sweet wine. All flesh shall know that I, the Lord, am your Savior,
And your Redeemer, the Mighty One of Jacob."*
**Isaiah 49:24-26**

# Acknowledgments

I THANK MY MAKER for the true man of God and ever-loving husband - Adebowale Bankole; you are greater than ten men put together. I appreciate you for being a solid pillar in this godly vision from the very beginning and for every word of encouragement you have spoken into my life. I am glad to be walking this path with you and our two precious gifts. You make it all worth it!

I also want to appreciate my dear pastors of many years for being there during my search for answers in the strange battles that led me to discover the power of deliverance. I thank the Almighty God for Pastors Wale and Foluke Akinosun. May the Lord enlarge your territory exceedingly and increase your unction to function in Jesus' name.

I appreciate the Lord for some of the generals that are not ashamed to teach and pray against the daily warfare that occurs in the spirit realm. Your examples gave me confidence that God is indeed a Man of War - Pastor Grace Okonrende and Prophetess Francina Norman. Your ministries not only touched my life but showed me how God uses women battle-axes!

As for Dr. Kay and Pastor May Ijisesan, you have both shown me what destiny helpers look like in the flesh. Keep raising champions for our King!

I sincerely appreciate the various teams that has made this publication a success - Dewalette Creations, GodKulture and Chuckstr Photography. Thank you all for the excellent work you do. The Lord will make you great like the House of David!

Finally, to the intercessors all over the world, keep the fire of His zeal ablaze. Your prayers availeth much!

# Contents

Foreword

DELIVERANCE IS NOT JUST the desire of our heavenly father for all His children; it is also His perfect will. The pages of the New Testament are very emphatic about God's commitment to the wholeness of His family. God has not changed one bit. His will as demonstrated in the life and ministry of Jesus remains the same. God wants His family on earth to be totally delivered from every form of bondage.

> **Matthew 15:21-28** - *Then Jesus went out from there and departed to the region of Tyre and Sidon. And behold, a woman of Canaan came from that region and cried out to Him, saying, "Have mercy on me, O Lord, Son of David! My daughter is severely demon-possessed." But He answered her not a word. And His disciples came and urged Him, saying, "Send her away, for she cries out after us." But He answered and said, "I was not sent except to the lost sheep of the house of Israel." Then she came and worshiped Him, saying, "Lord, help me!" But He answered and said, "It is not good to take the children's bread and throw it to the little dogs." And she said, "Yes, Lord, yet even the little dogs eat the crumbs which fall from their masters' table." Then Jesus answered and said to her, "O woman, great is your faith! Let it be to you as you desire." And her daughter was healed from that very hour. .*

In the passage above, we see how a woman of Canaan descent refused to let go where the healing of her daughter was concerned, in spite of the fact that it was not yet the dispensation to minister to people that are non-Jews. Jesus honored her faith and restored her child's health. Simply because she refused to give up in the face of hopelessness.

You and I are living in a far better dispensation. Deliverance and healing is for all. In fact, as a child of God, deliverance is your bread. You only need to learn how to receive it through the process of faith. I strongly believe that God has inspired the author to put this great piece together so that you can have the revelation of deliverance and ultimately possess what is yours.

God's commitment to healing and deliverance is as strong as ever. However, you and I need a revelation of His will before deliverance can become our reality. Doctrines of men have been developed over the years at the expense of the liberation of the saints. Opinions have been formed as a result of men's experiences to the detriment of God's people. It is sad to know that some of these ungodly ideologies have perpetrated through our pulpits for years and many denominations have embraced such teachings, which have done everything but express the mind of the author and the finisher of our faith.

The days of glorifying the works of Satan are over. God has no lessons to teach to the church through sicknesses and demonic oppressions. We already have the greatest teacher in the Holy Spirit and we definitely do not need to take suffering classes from Satan in form of demonic oppressions. Jesus suffered and died so that the church can live in victory over sin, sicknesses and all forms of satanic oppression.

Raeni, in this book has used her personal testimony based on the revelation of God's Word to clearly express God's commitment to a believer's deliverance. I trust God that this book will inspire your faith to take back whatsoever the enemy has stolen from you. Your day of deliverance is today. Don't wait for another day. The price has been paid already and it's high time you enjoyed the spoils of the victory that Jesus wrought for you.

**Dr. Kay Ijisesan**
**President, KingsWord Ministries International**

# Introduction

I AM WRITING to let you know that deliverance is meant for you! I do not know how long you have been searching for deliverance but the scripture is very clear about it. Every child of Zion is programmed for deliverance. Obadiah 1:17-18 says,

> ..."but upon mount Zion shall be deliverance and there shall be holiness; and the house of Jacob shall possess their possessions. And the house of Jacob shall be a fire and the house of Joseph a flame and the house of Esau for stubble, and they shall kindle in them and devour them; there shall not be any remaining of the house of Esau; for the Lord hath spoken it."

You can be delivered! God's plan for every believer is to be delivered and remain permanently delivered. Not only will you be delivered but also you will possess all that the enemy has stolen from you in Jesus' name. The thief comes to steal, kill and destroy but Jesus came so that you can have abundant life (John 10:10)! He also programmed you to deliver other people who are experiencing satanic oppression or demonic possession.

**Mark 16:17-18** - *And these signs will follow those who believe: In My name they will cast out demons; they will speak with* *new tongues; $^{18}$ they will take up serpents; and if they drink anything deadly, it will by no means hurt them; they will lay hands on the sick, and they will recover.*

There are many people who are depressed, oppressed, suppressed and distressed by the enemy. Who is the enemy? It is not your wicked step-mother from home or the witch in your village or the demonic high-priest in your community (though the enemy can manifest through any of these ones or use them to gain access your life). The true enemy and our common adversary is Satan the devil and his evil angels (demons) who do his biddings. I am writing this book because I have experienced spiritual warfare first-hand and I want to share my testimony of deliverance along with the strategies the Holy Spirit taught to me to win at the most crucial time of my life.

The Bible says in Proverbs 11:9b,

*But through* **knowledge** *the righteous will be* **delivered.**

And also in Proverbs 24:10,

*If you faint in the day of adversity, your strength is small.*

You need spiritual strength and the knowledge of God's Word to fight spiritual warfare. The Psalmist said that God teaches our fingers to fight and our hands to war (Psalm 144:1). There is a strategy to spiritual warfare and it is very important for every believer to learn these strategies because at new birth we were automatically enlisted into an existing battle. This battle started even before Adam came on the scene. It started when a created being decided he wanted to be greater than his creator and was thrown out of heaven.

This created being was Lucifer and he took many rebels with him that day. We will learn more about this villain and the Hero (JESUS), whom the Creator used to disgrace him (the devil) completely.

Throughout scriptures we see that warfare was a common occurrence in the lives of God's people. As long as the devil remains man's archenemy, warfare will be a constant occurrence. The only difference between Bible days and now is that our warfare is more covert than overt; it takes place more in the spiritual realm than in the physical realm. Many people are not aware of the spiritual warfare around them each day and even if aware, many do not know how to wage this war. The enemy has also updated his moral and ethical manual so as not to appear so bloodthirsty but this is only a trick. The warfare is still as intense as ever, especially in the mind of man and sometimes in territorial spheres.

The scriptures make it clear that life is a war. However, we do not wage war against flesh and blood but against principalities (Ephesians 6:12). But Jesus said all powers have been given to Him and He has bestowed it to us.

> **Luke 10:19** - *Jesus said that he has given us power and authority over serpents and scorpions and over all the power of darkness.*

Since this battle is a spiritual battle, and we as believers have been automatically enlisted in the battle, we need to know how to fight and be totally delivered from every oppression and deception of the devil. My prayer is that you will be filled with the revelation required for your freedom.

**2 Corinthians 10:3-5** - *For though we walk in the flesh, we do not* war *according to the flesh. For the weapons of our warfare are not carnal but mighty in God for pulling down strongholds, casting down arguments and every high thing that exalts itself against the knowledge of God, bringing every thought into captivity to the obedience of Christ.*

# *My Personal Testimony* 1

MY PERSONAL LESSON about spiritual warfare started like a joke after I had my 2nd child in July 2008. Exactly eight days after she was born I experienced a full-blown panic attack for the first time in my life. I was extremely weak, losing a lot of blood at an alarming rate. I also had a headache that won't go away; it was bursting at the very center of my head, like I was carrying a very heavy load that was crushingly present but invisible. My husband had to call 911 when I started gasping for breath. I began to see the walls and the ceiling of my house open up as if it was time to exit my body. I felt my spirit floating out of my body.

After a few minutes, the paramedics came and drove me in an ambulance to the hospital. It was the most gruesome ride of my life. Up until that time, I had never experienced anything like that and I know I will never experience such again Jesus' name! I sincerely thought my time was up, but for some strange reason I could not let go. I kept screaming out scriptures and calling on Jesus. The paramedics tested me and every test came back normal – my blood pressure, temperature and even my pulse were normal – which was weird given the way my heart was bursting in my chest.

At the emergency room, they ran another battery of tests and all my vitals and other test results came back normal as well. That night, the ER doctor diagnosed me with panic attack. I was furious and very disappointed. My thought was, "I almost died and all you can come up with is panic attack?" The entire week was an intense battle for my life and I thank God for some intercessors that stood by my family during this extremely challenging season. I thought it was just a momentary affliction. The doctor even called it "baby blues" but one thing I did not know was that that night was the beginning of a five-year battle with an aggressive spirit of anxiety and depression.

The journey to different doctors began. I began searching for answers, getting second, third and fourth opinions. I was placed on all the medications for psychological disorders in the books for sleep – Paxil, Zoloft, Lexapro, Klonopin, Cymbalta, Xanax and Trazadone. I was placed on all kinds of psychotropic medication and none worked. Some doctors got frustrated with me either because I kept asking questions or they thought I was pretending. Over the course of the illness, the doctors ran different tests like the MRI of the brain, PET scan of the brain, CT scan of the abdomen and ultrasound scans to detect any problem with my internal organs. I even ended up doing several gynecology tests and a colonoscopy because the doctors weren't sure what to look for anymore.

Finally in July 2012, I wound up with a psychiatrist who added more medications that brought on more health complications through their side effects. There was a time my eyes would suddenly start twitching or my body would just start jerking and my hand would start trembling. I was also not sleeping at all and I had major nightmares. There were also moments where I would hear voices in my head saying things like, "Why don't you just park your car and jump into that pond?" During that time, I would get only an hour's sleep in 96 hours for weeks on end. This condition persisted over a 4-month period in the final year of the attack.

When the temperature was extremely hot on a summer day, I would shake uncontrollably like a leaf hanging from a tree. When it became very chilly in the winter, I would feel be burning heat from within. I really thought I was going to die but one day after over four years, a guest minister came to my church and revealed that it was a demonic attack, during a personal counseling session with her. She said that rituals carried out by some witchcraft forces triggered it. I became very angry and started a 21-day fast immediately with aggressive prayers. The Lord delivered me completely from the affliction and since October 2012 I stopped using all the psychotropic medications. Then I thought, "If that intensity of fire delivered me from the panic attacks, then I had better maintain that intensity of fire on my prayer altar." Till today, the Lord enables me to pray and fast at least 3 days a week with personal worship and night vigil sessions. Like Lester Sumrall said, "Flies cannot land on a hot stove". I have found that to be true. That experience has made me grow wild in unspeakable places! My praise is wild, my prayer is crazy and my service to His kingdom is out of this world!

Depression is usually chronic low-grade sadness. It is characterized by no excitement about things that would normally excite you, hopelessness, helplessness, low energy, too much or too little sleep, isolation from people, negative thoughts, emotional pain that never goes away accompanied with suicidal ideation and excessive preoccupation of death, lack of appetite or over eating and very low self esteem. At least, that is what the psychology textbooks describe and these symptoms remain a fact but the truth is that there is a spirit involved and it is called the spirit of heaviness and needs to be dealt with.

From Isaiah 61:3, we can see that an exchange can be made for the spirit of heaviness:

> *To console those who mourn in Zion,*
> *To give them beauty for ashes,*
> *The oil of joy for mourning,*
> *The garment of praise for the spirit of heaviness;*
> *That they may be called trees of righteousness,*
> *The planting of the* LORD, *that He may be glorified.*

The spirit of heaviness needs to be dealt with aggressively through praise and must be cast out as a demonic spirit. Like a friend rightly describes it, it is "a cloud that envelops you". As a pastor or leader in ministry, please make sure you are speaking to the oppressed person with compassion but addressing the spirit of heaviness as a different entity like Jesus dealt ruthlessly with demonic spirits. People who are fighting depression are already at their lowest point emotionally and mentally; be careful not to attribute the cause of their emotional pain to the person but to the spirit involved.

Nobody enjoys depression and the truth is that the spirit of heaviness is clouding his or her judgments already. Regardless of how the depression came to be, be kind to the person but ruthless with the demon. Please do not use words like "Stop wallowing in self-pity" or "You are so sad because you have forgotten how to be thankful". I have seen well-meaning people tell me things like:, "Why are you so afraid on the plane? People die in their sleep everyday." The minute those kinds of words are released, the demons torment the person with the idea of dying in their sleep so much that they completely lose the will to sleep.

While depression generally slows people down, panic attacks aggravate people emotionally and mentally, mimicking heart attacks – your heart races, your palms sweat, your fingers and toes grow numb and cold; you become extremely fearful and sometimes black out. You may begin to see intense light or extreme darkness. The experience leaves you drained with exhaustion and dizziness. It is like being tormented by the spirit of death over and over again. I sincerely believe these are the work of demonic spirits. The headaches start at the center of the head and spread like a rotating sprinkler. It is accompanied by extreme tiredness and excruciating body aches with high- or low-grade fever. Gradually, the feeling of malady degenerates to the point of extreme discomfort, loss of sleep and then loss of appetite.

The final stage is usually complete loss of muscle tone and extreme fear characterized by cold resulting in shaking, numbness of the fingers and toes. There is a major foreboding of impending danger or fear of death and these feelings persist and linger despite the use of medication. The medications are a different kind of sickness altogether because of their side effects. The nature of the attack is so severe that by the time you read the instruction pamphlet that come with your prescription (which is typical in the United States) describing the side effects and contra-indications, you will experience all the symptoms listed on the paper one by one. It is almost as if the demons can read too. It became so bad that my way of coping was not to read any of the pamphlets that came with the medications. The principal demon that afflicts in panic attack is a spirit of "fear" accompanied with some others like confusion and partial loss of memory.

There was also this unbelievable pain on the lower left side of my back, just in the slight arch of my back. It radiates throughout the body. It's almost as if this part of my body knows when I am happy, sad, tired or weak. It feels everything. All these symptoms and all the doctors can say is - panic attack but they couldn't explain the cause or reason for the back pain. One doctor even began to suggest kidney problems and another thought it was fibromyalgia. I think it is the work of devils and either the doctors are completely clueless and don't have any idea what they are up against or they are too arrogant to admit they don't know how to handle it! My curiosity was confirmed when I came across a book called "Spiritual Warfare: Fighting demons by Scott Meade. The author described a pressure on the back as the presence of demons. Years later, I understood it was a nest of the demon of affliction similar to the case of the woman bent over by a spirit of affliction in the Bible that had her bound for 18 years and Jesus Christ set her completely free instantly. He is still in the business of setting people free!

> **Luke 13:11-13** - *And behold, there was a woman who had a spirit of infirmity eighteen years, and was bent over and could in no way raise herself up.* [12] *But when Jesus saw her, He called her to Him and said to her, "Woman, you are loosed from your infirmity."* [13] *And He laid His hands on her, and immediately she was made straight, and glorified God.*

In verse 16 Jesus attributed the attack to the devil;

> *So ought not this woman, being a daughter of Abraham, whom*

*Satan has bound—think of it—for eighteen years, be loosed from this bond on the Sabbath?*

This strange condition was usually triggered by bad or sad news even on the mass media. I avoided listening to the national news like a plague for a really long time because after everyone went to bed, I would still be awake with the recycling thoughts like semis (trailers) driving through my mind at break neck speed. For example the ill-fated Dana airline plane crash that happened in Nigeria in May of 2012 was a major trigger compounded by the death of a loved one. Within the week the news broke, I was passing out and fainting by any little provocation. It was really bad, it was like living on the edge of a cliff. This wicked spirit of affliction dealt with me and the crisis led to a huge change in my life. Toward the end of 2012, as I was struggling with keeping my sanity and stamina, more tragic news came.

A young precious woman of God was terminally ill and passed on within a very short time. This news particularly shook me because this was one of the few people that understood what had been going on in my life over the last few years. It was during this period that I received complete healing and deliverance from the Lord because I became desperate for answers. I got angry at the devil and went on a rampage against sickness. I started with a personal 21-day fasting and prayer journey during which the Holy Spirit himself showed me the secret of deliverance through the Word, prayer and fervent praise.

You can get answers to your situation too. God is not a partial God! I have found out that He is able to fulfill all His promises. He promised you long life, you cannot die young.

He promised you good health, you will not be sick in Jesus' name. He said you are empowered for success: you cannot be a failure anymore. I believe that God has spared my life to share my testimony to encourage you and let you know that Jehovah heals. In 2 Corinthians 1:3-4 Paul the Apostle said,

> *Blessed be the God and Father of our Lord Jesus Christ, the Father of mercies and God of all comfort, who comforts us in all our tribulation, that we may be able to comfort those who are in any trouble, with the comfort with which we ourselves are comforted by God.*

Going through this particular tribulation and overcoming has given credence to God's faithfulness. The Lord wants His children to be well and He is still the Great Physician. There is so many promises in the Holy Scriptures that show His will concerning our health. Many of those verses helped me through the time of intense battle and still remain my shield in the day of trouble. Some of the nuggets I discovered in the Holy Scriptures are listed at the back of this book for different areas of application. God is Omniscient and His works are replicable in any given situation. If it worked for me, it can work for you! He is the same yesterday, today and forever more.

## YOU DON'T HAVE TO EXPERIENCE SICKNESS TO MINISTER TO THE SICK!

I must say at this juncture that even though I experienced sickness firsthand, you don't have to experience sickness or affliction to be able to deliver others. As a believer, it is part of your responsibility and mission to lay hands on the sick and they will recover. You may just be a reader of this book who is a minister and simply wants to understand how to defeat the enemy in the lives of others. You are taking a very vital step in acquiring the knowledge you need because 2 Timothy 2:15 says,

> *Study and be eager and do your utmost to present yourself to God approved (tested by trial), a workman who has no cause to be ashamed, correctly analyzing and accurately dividing [rightly handling and skillfully teaching] the Word of Truth. (AMP)*

Some people believe that you must go through a particular affliction before you can teach others with authority about the any particular topic. I will say not really, I don't believe a Christian has to go through all types of trial to be able to minister to all but you will definitely go through your own specific trial. For example Paul went through many trials but never got married and he was able to teach about marriage by the Spirit of the Lord.

My favorite explanation for teaching by the Spirit of the Lord is described in 1 Corinthians 2 and it really confirms what Job 32:8 was saying about the spirit in man that gives understanding. I truly believe God permits those different trials to groom us character-wise. A teacher of the word once said that "miracles don't grow you but trials do". Even Jesus though He was a son, learned obedience through the things which He suffered (Hebrews 5:8). Many believers will teach others through their personal testimonies and many will also be able to teach as by the Spirit of the Lord. I don't think you can possibly experience all the types of affliction under the sun except in peculiar cases like Job; his tribulation touched every single area of his life but you cannot have one without the other.

As a Christian, you will learn some things by experience through trials peculiar to your journey and you will also learn some deep truths by the spirit of the Lord. I believe that the latter is best for every one of us. Check out most experienced teachers of the word; their testimonies are impactful; the bigger the trial the greater the testimony. For example, I battled with clinical depression and anxiety attacks for about 5 years and the latter part of 2012, I was critically ill and the doctors ran all manner of tests but came short but God showed up. I understand spiritual warfare a little and I'm still learning. After I received complete healing many people with different manner of diagnosis and mis-diagnosis have been blessed, encouraged and received their own healing from the testimony of my healing. Mine was in the area of my health; others may be in their finances, marriage, childbearing or career. Most times we don't see the reason for trials as believers and many take shortcuts out of the process ending us as half-baked child/son but the best of God's generals are forged in the furnace of trials. Please look through the popular "hall of faith" in Hebrews 11:1-end. Everyone there passed through fiery trials and ended up with exceeding great testimonies.

**REFLECTION:**
*Father Lord, give me a testimony of complete deliverance. Let the world gather to hear me declare your glory.*

# 2
# Sons, Not Children

SPIRITUAL WARFARE IS for sons and not children! Children are not equipped to fight for themselves and that is why the Lord placed children in the care of their parents till they mature. Paul speaking in 1 Corinthians 13:11 said,

> *When I was a child, I spoke as a child, I understood as a child, I thought as a child; but when I became a man, I put away childish things.*

There is a need to mature (grow up) in the things of God. One way to grow up is by studying the Word of God and praying with the written Word. When the enemy came against Jesus in Matthew 4, He kept fighting back with the written Word of God, which is also the sword of the spirit. The Bible says the world is waiting for the manifestation of sons (Romans 8:19). Children don't manifest; only sons do! Little children are saved but do not have the capacity to match the enemy in warfare but young men do and fathers have become experts that can equip others in spiritual warfare. It is expedient that you grow in the knowledge of the Holy One if you don't want the devil to molest you. 1 John 2:14 says,

*I have written to you, fathers, Because you have known Him who is from the beginning. I have written to you, young men, Because you are strong, and the word of God abides in you, And you have overcome the wicked one.*

If you really want to actualize your destiny in Christ Jesus, then it is time to celebrate spiritual warfare. It is almost impossible to avoid trials because it is the boxing ring of champions. James 1:2-4 says,

*My brethren, **count it all joy** when you fall into various **trials**, knowing that the testing of your faith produces patience. But let patience have its perfect work, that you may be perfect and complete, lacking nothing.*

I love Galatians 4:1-5 so much because it clearly depicts the difference between a son and a child:

*Now I say that the heir, as long as he is a child, does not differ at all from a slave, though he is master of all, ² but is under guardians and stewards until the time appointed by the father. ³ Even so we, when we were children, were in bondage under the elements of the world. ⁴ But when the fullness of the time had come, God sent forth His Son, born of a woman, born under the law, ⁵ to redeem those who were under the law, that we might receive the adoption as sons.*

The same is foretold about the Messiah in Isaiah 9:6,

*Unto us a child is born but unto is a son is given.*

Jesus could not die for our sins until He became a son. When He was a child His parents fled with Him from Herod but when He became a son, He confronted Herod without fear.

Trials don't break us; they actually make us. Trials make you grow wild in unspeakable places! My praise is wild, my prayer is crazy and my service to His kingdom is out of this world! Why? Because I understand that the enemy keeps attacking the treasure – the assignment or your specific area of calling.

I once heard of a very young lady who was attacked by the enemy with cancer in her lungs because she played all kinds of wind instruments like the trumpet, saxophone and flute. She was a believer and had never smoked in her entire life but the enemy attacked her specific area of gifting. You must not be ignorant of the devices of the evil one. The prince of this world is the thief from the beginning who has come to steal, kill and destroy (John 10:10a). It has been revealed over and again in scriptures (from the Garden of Eden in Genesis through the final wars in the book of revelations) that he is after the possession of man.

The enemy is very territorial about the earth and man's dominion over it. He will fight tooth and nail to possess and dominate in every possible way. He is greedy for possession and power. Remember the contest he had with The Master Himself in the wilderness in Matthew 4:8-10, where he wanted to bribe the Possessor of heaven and earth with material wealth in exchange for His dominion. See the scripture below:

**Matthew 4:8** - *Again, the devil took Him up on an exceedingly high mountain, and showed Him all the kingdoms of the world and their glory. ⁹ And he said to Him, "All these things I will give You if You will fall down and worship me." ¹⁰ Then Jesus said to him, "Away with you, Satan! For it is written, 'You shall worship the LORD your God, and Him only you shall serve.'*

Satan's attacks are always about your possession and your power (dominion). The enemy is in the business of grabbing power and the Master is in the business of bestowing power. Look at the illustration painted in scriptures by Jesus Himself about demonic oppression, the strongman and his possession in Luke 11:20-26:

> But if I cast out demons with the finger of God, surely the kingdom of God has come upon you. ²¹ When a strong man, fully armed, guards his own palace, his goods are in peace. ²² But when a stronger than he comes upon him and overcomes him, he takes from him all his armor in which he trusted, and divides his spoils. ²³ He who is not with Me is against Me, and he who does not gather with Me scatters. ²⁴ When an unclean spirit goes out of a man, he goes through dry places, seeking rest; and finding none, he says, 'I will return to my house from which I came.' ²⁵ And when he comes, he finds it swept and put in order. ²⁶ Then he goes and takes with him seven other spirits more wicked than himself, and they enter and dwell there; and the last state of that man is worse than the first.

If you are barren, jobless, failing in academic or professional pursuit, broke, stagnated, sick with or without medical explanation, mentally ill, depressed, terminally sick, genetically ill, single past your prime, hated without cause, working but having little or nothing to show for it, under constant attack in your dream, suffering insomnia, suffering from addiction, prayerlessness, praying without results, experiencing marital failure - YOU ARE PROBABLY UNDER THE ATTACK OF THE ENEMY! You are most likely experiencing spiritual attack. You need to change your gear! The Bible says that if your strength fails in the days of adversity then your strength is small (Proverbs 24:10). You must pray some prayers of enquiry like David in 1 Samuel 30:8,

> *So David inquired of the* **Lord***, saying, "Shall I* **pursue**
> *this troop? Shall I overtake them?" And He answered him,*
> ***"Pursue***, *for you shall surely overtake them and without fail*
> **recover** *all.*

You must seriously evaluate your life like Jabez and you must
pray through to break through like Hannah. Your name must
change like Jacob who was called cheater or supplanter, but
after he wrestled through the night he emerged a prince in the
morning.

## SIN: A DOORWAY

There must also be no anchor for the enemy to operate in your
life. Give no place to the devil. Do not allow him any foothold
at all because the foothold usually becomes a stronghold.

You cannot afford any ungodly habit nor indulge in any hidden
sin. You cannot toy with anger, resentment, bitterness or
unforgiveness. Not only will they impede your prayer, they will
also leave you exposed to the enemy. In Zechariah 3:1-5, the
enemy was able to resist him Joshua, despite the fact that he
was the high priest standing before God, purely because of his
filthy garment. What is your filthy garment? Wash it now in the
blood of Jesus. Don't procrastinate at all. Begin to mention the
sins, habits or issues of resentments as the Holy Spirit brings
them to your remembrance. Your spouse may not know it, your
pastor may only see your spiritual side, your family members
may be fooled, but God sees and the enemy knows! Confess
and renounce them now.

One of the doorways of demonic attack or oppression in a Christian's life is through sin, especially the shame and guilt that weakens your defenses as a child of God. The condemnation that strips you of the important ingredient needed to resist the devil – your faith!

**1 John 5:4** - *For whatever is born of God overcomes the world. And this is the victory that has overcome the world—our faith.*

I am not proud of some things I did in the past. For the benefit of someone reading this book, I must share some of it. There was a sin I secretly indulged in from my youth (masturbation) and revisited one more time in my marriage, unknown to my husband. I made excuses that it was only once and justified it because of some wrong counsel I got from fellow Christians and popular media – the lie that masturbation is not a sin but an avenue to relieve pent up desires. It was a secret sin that I had engaged in from my teenage years; it was temporarily gratifying like what Hebrews 11:25 described as fleeting pleasures of sin but I usually felt awfully filthy afterwards. This was only a tip of the iceberg! The enormity of this sin was that it opened me up to several demons that oppressed and tormented by body for many years until I denounced the sin, confessed it and got delivered completely from the spirit of perversion.

After much study and research, I discovered that this unclean spirit or demon of perversion manifests through the fingers during deliverance. If you are struggling with masturbation or any form of sexual perversion, seek help quickly because these demons take control of many lives, especially using secrecy as a tool. If you are a young person reading this book, please DO NOT toy with masturbation! It is a foul spirit that opens the doorway to other more wicked spirits like Jesus mentioned in

Luke 11:24-26,

> *When an unclean spirit goes out of a man, he goes through dry places, seeking rest; and finding none, he says, 'I will return to my house from which I came.'* [25] *And when he comes, he finds it swept and put in order.* [26] *Then he goes and takes with him seven other spirits more wicked than himself, and they enter and dwell there; and the last state of that man is worse than the first.*

Many people classify this sin as harmless and so unknowingly classify the spirit behind it as harmless too. The only danger is that as easily and as many times you cast out this unclean spirit, it will keep bringing back more wicked spirits than itself to inhabit the transgressor. So before you indulge in that act of masturbation again, remember the more wicked counterparts controlling things like pornography on the internet, x-rated movies and erotic books, fornication, adultery and sexual immorality in general. Spirits with similar activity tend to roll together e.g. someone manifesting pride will almost always have anger and bitterness, and someone who is greedy will be very selfish as well. If you or someone in your life is manifesting any of these behaviors without control or is addicted to anything, a demonic spirit is probably involved.

## ANOTHER DOORWAY: ANGER

> **Ephesians 6:26-27** - *Be angry, and do not sin: do not let the sun go down on your wrath,* [27] **nor give place to the devil.**

Another doorway that I let the enemy use to gain access into my life was the spirit of anger – uncontrollable anger or sudden outburst of rage. It is listed in Galatians 5:19 as part of the works of the flesh. It was like unleashing a dam of bottled up frustration and wrath. It was never pretty. I had internalized anger throughout my teenage years when a false prophet that my parents consulted with wrongfully accused me of having performed an abortion. I was brutally punished for the sin that I never committed and so I became withdrawn and extremely vindictive, holding grudges against anyone who dared to cross my path.

Most of my adolescence and young adult years, I was a ticking time bomb waiting to erupt. I later discovered in graduate school that clinical depression is also known as reverted or internalized anger usually bottled up because there was no way to express it or help yourself when victimized by a force bigger than you. Hence the term "learned helplessness". As I had earlier mentioned, I was diagnosed with dysthymic – chronic low-grade depression but got delivered completely by confessing the sin of anger and I had to forgive all the people involved in the trauma that led to it. I truly believe that what the Bible refers to as the spirit of heaviness in Isaiah 61:3 is what popular culture is calling depression today and it is plaguing the society from early childhood through old age.

Depression, anger, rage, lying and the likes are the works of the flesh – the nature of the old man, the fallen nature. Galatians 5:9 says a little leaven, leavens the whole lump. I have openly confessed my own sins. What is yours? Look through the list in Galatians 5:19 to identify whatever the enemy could be using against you. Go ahead now and confess it to the Lord. If you remember more tomorrow, go on your knees and confess each one also knowing that God is faithful and just to forgive you (1 John 1:9). Gain right standing before God because you really need it to engage effectively in spiritual warfare.

Whether you feel condemnation or boldness to approach

before the Lord is not relevant because Christ died and gave you a gift called RIGHTEOUSNESS but the enemy knows how to torment and weaken the Christian with the fear that comes from condemnation. So I thank God Almighty for Romans 8:1 which says that there now no condemnation to those who are in Christ Jesus who walk not after the flesh. The good thing about confessing the sin to the Lord is that it helps you bear your chest and removes the power of condemnation after the Holy Spirit has convicted you.

Conviction comes from the Holy Spirit and it is liberating but condemnation is from the devil and it brings bondage. Hebrews 4:16 says to approach His throne with boldness and obtain grace in the time of need. Run to the Lord for cover!

## GRACE

You will need abundant grace in this warfare. The Bible says in Romans 6:14,

> *For sin shall not have dominion over you, for you are not under law but under grace.*

The scriptures also reiterates in Ephesians 2:4-6,

> *But God, who is rich in mercy, because of His great love with which He loved us, ⁵ even when we were dead in trespasses, made us alive together with Christ (by grace you have been saved), ⁶ and raised us up together, and made us sit together in the heavenly places in Christ Jesus.*

You should also know that you are seated far above all the powers of darkness in all their diabolical ranks according to Ephesians 1:19-21,

*And what is the exceeding greatness of His power toward us who believe, according to the working of His mighty power [20] which He worked in Christ when He raised Him from the dead and seated Him at His right hand in the heavenly places, [21] far above all principality and power and might and dominion, and every name that is named, not only in this age but also in that which is to come".*

First you must be on the Lord's side. If God be for us who can be against us but if God be against you, who can deliver you out of His hands? Get right with God first. If you are not born again, get saved. If you were saved and have now backslidden, then you must re-dedicate your life to God right now. In spiritual warfare you cannot afford to sit on the fence. Its either you are in or out! If you are undecided, you can become a casualty of war from either side. You may receive someone else's arrow and that is dangerous. You can only get divine covering if you have been translated to the kingdom of His marvelous light. One way that I check if someone is saved is by asking him or her candidly, "If you die today or the rapture happens, are you sure you will go to heaven?" If they are not sure, I usually just advice that they become sure by giving their lives to Christ. Please if you do not have the assurance of faith, kindly say this prayer quickly.

**PRAYER:**
*Lord Jesus, I come to You today knowing that I am a sinner. Please forgive me my sins and wash me with Your precious blood. I accept You as my Lord and Savior. Now I know that I am born again. Your grace has found me today; please let it keep me till the day of reckoning. Thank you Lord for saving me. Amen.*

## CASTING OUT DEMONS:

You can cast out evil spirits with the authority in the name of Jesus by taking these easy steps.

1. Confess the sin that open the door to the demonic oppression or possession.
2. Renounce the demon and its activity and cast it out.
3. Command the demon to never return in Jesus' name.
4. Cover person or area with the blood of Jesus and Holy Ghost fire.
5. You can also apply the anointing oil (James 5:14, Isaiah 10:27).

I encourage you to engage in praise warfare and fasting with aggressive prayers. It is not the typical hunger strike that will expel this level of affliction but intense and specific prayer and fasting like Jesus mentioned in Matthew 17:14-21,

> *And when they had come to the multitude, a man came to Him, kneeling down to Him and saying, *15* "Lord, have mercy on my son, for he is an epileptic and suffers severely; for he often falls into the fire and often into the water. *16* So I brought him to Your disciples, but they could not cure him."*17* Then Jesus answered and said, "O faithless and perverse generation, how long shall I be with you? How long shall I bear with you? Bring him here to Me." *18* And Jesus rebuked the demon, and it came out of him; and the child was cured from that very hour. *19* Then the disciples came to Jesus privately and said, "Why could we not cast it out?" *20* So Jesus said to them, "Because of your unbelief; for assuredly, I say to you, if you have faith as a mustard seed, you will say to this mountain, 'Move from here to there,' and it will move; and nothing will be impossible for you. *21* However, this kind does not go out except by prayer and fasting."*

Before I go into details about the tool that Christ Jesus mentioned in Matthew 17:21 for expelling demons, you need to understand where they come from. Please see Chapter 5 for a detailed study about the origin of demons.

**REFLECTION**:
*Father Lord, give me the grace to mature into son-ship so that I can manifest your glory to the entire world.*

# 3
# The Angelic Host

THE LORD OF HOST is the head of the angelic host and His angels are sent to protect us and minister to all our needs. They defend God's people in deep spiritual warfare. For example, in 2 Kings 19, a wicked king came against Hezekiah to threaten him and destroy the land. The entire nation cried out to God in prayer and the Lord sent a militant angel to defend His own. See verse 35 below:

> *And it came to pass on a certain night that the angel of the Lord went out, and killed in the camp of the Assyrians one hundred and eighty-five thousand; and when people arose early in the morning, there were the corpses—all dead.*

Are you going through a strange battle? Do not be afraid or dismayed, the Lord God still has angels who defends and protects His people. Psalms 103:20 confirms that these angels excel in strength and hearken to the voice of His words. You can provoke angelic intervention by praying according to scriptures. There are different types of angels and I believe they are organized in ranks like the military. Can you imagine that God in His infinite wisdom would not put a strategic order in place among the angelic host? Our God is a God of divine order and the order mimicked by the rulers of darkness was copied from the original.

## GOD'S ANGELS

Angels are heavenly beings created by God to worship Him and protect or minister to the heirs of salvation. To minister simply means they are to meet our needs.

> **Hebrews 1:7, 14** - *And of the angels He says: "Who makes His angels spirits And His ministers a flame of fire. <sup>14</sup> Are they not all ministering spirits sent forth to minister for those who will inherit salvation?*

They are spirit beings who are not visible in our physical realm but sometimes appear to God's people for specific purposes. They usually serve as divine messengers between God and his people like the Angel Gabriel who announced the birth of Jesus to His mother Mary.

> **Luke 1:26-33** - *Now in the sixth month the angel Gabriel was sent by God to a city of Galilee named Nazareth, <sup>27</sup> to a virgin betrothed to a man whose name was Joseph, of the house of David. The virgin's name was Mary. <sup>28</sup> And having come in, the angel said to her, "Rejoice, highly favored one, the Lord is with you; blessed are you among women!" <sup>29</sup> But when she saw him, she was troubled at his saying, and considered what manner of greeting this was. <sup>30</sup> Then the angel said to her, "Do not be afraid, Mary, for you have found favor with God. <sup>31</sup> And behold, you will conceive in your womb and bring forth a Son, and shall call His name JESUS. <sup>32</sup> He will be great, and will be called the Son of the Highest; and the Lord God will give Him the throne of His father David. <sup>33</sup> And He will reign over the house of Jacob forever, and of His kingdom there will be no end."*

The angels of the Lord also serve as guardians or protective security agents or bodyguards for God's children. When the children of Israel left the land of Egypt after 430 years, the Bible records that all the armies of the Lord left Egypt that day,

> **Exodus 12:41** - *And it came to pass at the end of the four hundred and thirty years—on that very same day—it came to pass that all the armies of the Lord went out from the land of Egypt.*

I don't think the **Armies of the Lord** here was talking about the people alone but the angelic army. If you look up this verse of scripture in other translations you will see the different words used for the word *army* – forces, host, and divisions. These words can hardly be used to describe slaves that have been subdued by a satanic principality for centuries. The Lord of Host – the Captain of the angelic armies – sent out His entourage that day to accompany the oppressed out of bondage! See how the angel ministered to the prophet in a time of distress in 1 Kings 19:4-8,

> *But he himself went a day's journey into the wilderness, and came and sat down under a broom tree. And he prayed that he might die, and said, "It is enough! Now, Lord, take my life, for I am no better than my fathers!" Then as he lay and slept under a broom tree, suddenly an angel touched him, and said to him, "Arise and eat." Then he looked, and there by his head was a cake baked on coals, and a jar of water. So he ate and drank, and lay down again. And the angel of the Lord came back the second time, and touched him, and said, "Arise and eat, because the journey is too great for you." So he arose, and ate and drank; and he went in the strength of that food forty days and forty nights as far as Horeb, the mountain of God.*

# EVERY CHURCH HAS AN ANGEL

Do you know that every church has an angel assigned to it? See how the angel of the church aided and fought for the church when prayer intensified in Acts 12:1-24,

> *Now about that time Herod the king stretched out his hand to harass some from the church. Then he killed James the brother of John with the sword. And because he saw that it pleased the Jews, he proceeded further to seize Peter also. Now it was during the Days of Unleavened Bread. So when he had arrested him, he put him in prison, and delivered him to four squads of soldiers to keep him, intending to bring him before the people after Passover. Peter was therefore kept in prison, but constant prayer was offered to God for him by the church. And when Herod was about to bring him out, that night Peter was sleeping, bound with two chains between two soldiers; and the guards before the door were keeping the prison. Now behold, an **angel** of the Lord stood by him, and a light shone in the prison; and he struck Peter on the side and raised him up, saying, "Arise quickly!" And his chains fell off his hands. Then the angel said to him, "Gird yourself and tie on your sandals"; and so he did. And he said to him, "Put on your garment and follow me." So he went out and followed him, and did not know that what was done by the angel was real, but thought he was seeing a vision. When they were past the first and the second guard posts, they came to the iron gate that leads to the city, which opened to them of its own accord; and they went out and went down one street, and immediately the **angel** departed from him. And when Peter had come to himself, he said, "Now I know for certain that the Lord has sent His **angel**, and has delivered me from the hand of Herod and from all the expectation of the Jewish people." So, when he had considered this, he came to the house of Mary, the mother of John whose surname was Mark, where*

*many were gathered together praying. And as Peter knocked at the door of the gate, a girl named Rhoda came to answer. When she recognized Peter's voice, because of her gladness she did not open the gate, but ran in and announced that Peter stood before the gate. But they said to her, "You are beside yourself!" Yet she kept insisting that it was so. So they said, "It is his* **angel***." Now Peter continued knocking; and when they opened the door and saw him, they were astonished. But motioning to them with his hand to keep silent, he declared to them how the Lord had brought him out of the prison. And he said, "Go, tell these things to James and to the brethren." And he departed and went to another place. Then, as soon as it was day, there was no small stir among the soldiers about what had become of Peter. But when Herod had searched for him and not found him, he examined the guards and commanded that they should be put to death. And he went down from Judea to Caesarea, and stayed there. Now Herod had been very angry with the people of Tyre and Sidon; but they came to him with one accord, and having made Blastus the king's personal aide their friend, they asked for peace, because their country was supplied with food by the king's country. So on a set day Herod, arrayed in royal apparel, sat on his throne and gave an oration to them. And the people kept shouting, "The voice of a god and not of a man!" Then immediately an* **angel** *of the Lord struck him, because he did not give glory to God. And he was eaten by worms and died. But the word of God grew and multiplied.*

Prayer moves God's angels into action. Praying according to scripture strengthens your angels in warfare.

**Psalm 103:20** - *Bless the Lord, you His angels, Who excel in strength, who do His word, Heeding the voice of His word.*

# ANGELIC RANKS OR ORDER

1. **Cherubim**: I would rather have the cherubim accompany me than a legion of the most sophisticated armies! The Bible mentioned cherubim right from the book of beginnings when Adam and Eve fell and were evicted from the Garden of Eden.

> **Genesis 3:24** - *So He drove out the man; and He placed* **cherubim** *at the east of the Garden of Eden, and a flaming sword which turned every way, to guard the way to the tree of life.*

These angels are fierce-looking to show that God meant business! God Himself sits enthroned above the Cherubim (Psalm 99:1) and rides out to warfare on the wheels of the Cherubim. See their description in Ezekiel 10:20-21,

> *This is the living creature [of four combined creatures] that I saw beneath the God of Israel by the river Chebar, and I knew that they were cherubim. ²¹ Each one had four faces and each one had four wings, and what looked like the hands of a man was under their wings.*

There is an amazing depiction of the cherubim in scriptures – the angelic beings who cover the throne of God.

2. **Seraphim**: These strange beings are different from the cherubim and were mentioned only once in the scriptures as seen in the vision of the prophet Isaiah in Isaiah 6:2,

> *Above Him stood the seraphim; each had six wings: with two [each] covered his [own] face, and with two [each] covered his feet, and with two [each] flew. ³ And one cried to another and*

*said, Holy, holy, holy is the Lord of hosts; the whole earth is full of His glory! (AMP)*

Their name literally means the "burning ones" with brilliant light from emanating within them and they are in charge of guarding God's throne.

3. **Archangels**: These are captains of different angelic hosts and are also known to bring messages from the throne room of God to mankind. The examples of archangels are shown throughout scriptures with some of their names mentioned like Michael and Gabriel. You can see a good demonstration of their task and rank when an angel was speaking to Daniel about how a principality called the prince of Persia withstood him in Daniel 10:13,

> *But the prince of the kingdom of Persia withstood me twenty-one days; and behold, Michael, one of the chief princes, came to help me, for I had been left alone there with the kings of Persia.*

*Chief* is another word for leader, head, captain or arch. In the spirit realm during spiritual warfare, the ranks have to match. The angelic prince of the kingdom of God was the only true match for the prince of the kingdom of darkness. These princes are also known as **principalities**. Remember that Christ Jesus (the Mighty Man of war) is the head of all principalities and powers.

**Other Ranks**: I sincerely believe that there are various ranks among this vast angelic host but I do not see where they are clearly listed in scriptures apart from the two below. They talk about thrones, dominions, principalities and powers in Colossians 1:16,

*For by Him all things were created that are in heaven and that are on earth, visible and invisible, whether thrones or dominions or **principalities** or powers. All things were created through Him and for Him.*

Some other ranks were mentioned as rulers and spiritual host in Ephesians 6:12:

*For we do not wrestle against flesh and blood, but against principalities, against powers, against the rulers of the darkness of this age, against spiritual hosts of wickedness in the heavenly places.*

Jesus addressed the angels of the churches in the book of revelation. It is my personal conviction that every church (no matter how big or small) has a lead angel assigned to it.

**Revelations 1:20** - *The mystery of the seven stars which you saw in My right hand, and the seven golden lampstands: The seven stars are the angels of the seven churches, and the seven lampstands which you saw are the seven churches.*

I also believe that every individual child of God has a guardian angel that ministers to his or needs constantly. They are usually invisible but they are revealed on special occasions when God's elect is in serious trouble, like in the case of Elijah fleeing Jezebel's wrath and was fed by the angel assigned to him (1 Kings 19) or the angel of Peter who broke him out of jail in Acts 12:5-10.

**Note:** I would like to mention that this book is not an exhaustive study of angels but only to provoke you to a more diligent search of the scriptures to understand spiritual warfare. I do not care what dungeon the enemy thought he has thrown you – there is a Master Jail-Breaker and His angels are still at work breaking chains of brass and fetters of iron.

**REFLECTION**:
*Father Lord, release your militant angelic host to fight all the strange battles arrayed against me in Jesus' name!*

# 4
# *The Satanic Host*

THE SATANIC HOST is led by none other than Satan himself aka Lucifer, the Accuser, the dragon, the serpent or the devil. Satan was an angel too. He was a covering cherub until iniquity was found in him according to Ezekiel 28:14-15:

> *You were the anointed cherub who covers; I established you; You were on the holy mountain of God; You walked back and forth in the midst of fiery stones. [15] You were perfect in your ways from the day you were created, Till iniquity was found in you.*

According to scriptures, he was also in the Garden of Eden reflecting perfection and serving the Almighty God. All was well until he committed the highest treason – he desired to become equal with God! He became too familiar with the Creator of the visible and invisible worlds. He was a good guy gone rogue and his name Lucifer meant "Light Bearer" and was also referred to as the son of the morning in Isaiah 14:12-15,

> *How you are fallen from heaven, O Lucifer, son of the morning!*

*How you are cut down to the ground,*
*You who weakened the nations!*
*¹³ For you have said in your heart:*
*'I will ascend into heaven,*
*I will exalt my throne above the stars of God;*
*I will also sit on the mount of the congregation*
*On the farthest sides of the north;*
*¹⁴ I will ascend above the heights of the clouds,*
*I will be like the Most High.'*
*¹⁵ Yet you shall be brought down to Sheol,*
*To the lowest depths of the Pit.*

## FALLEN ANGELS

When the devil rebelled against the God-head, he was thrown out of heaven with a third of the angelic host. They are not demons but this cohort became the fallen angels and formed the evil hierarchy that continually wages war against the seed of the woman. See the account in Revelation 12:7-12,

*And war broke out in heaven: Michael and his angels fought with the dragon; and the dragon and his angels fought, ⁸ but they did not prevail, nor was a place found for them in heaven any longer. ⁹ So the great dragon was cast out, that serpent of old, called the Devil and Satan, who deceives the whole world; he was cast to the earth, and his angels were cast out with him. ¹⁰ Then I heard a loud voice saying in heaven, "Now salvation, and strength, and the kingdom of our God, and the power of His Christ have come, for the accuser of our brethren, who accused them before our God day and night, has been cast down. ¹¹ And they overcame him by the blood of the Lamb and by the word of their testimony, and they did not love their lives to the death. ¹² Therefore rejoice O heavens, and you who dwell in them! Woe* to the inhabitants of the earth and the sea! For the devil has come down to you, having great wrath, because he knows that he has a short time."

If you read the preceding verses, you will get a full picture of what happened during that fall-out. Like any political rebellion, the villain didn't do it alone but dragged down a third of the angelic host with him and this is clearly stated in Revelation 12:4a,

His tail drew a third of the stars of heaven and threw them to the earth.

These angels became what we now know as the "fallen angels". They found it easy to copy the same order on the godly rank of angelic host and exert their power in all spheres of human existence. The devil is known as the prince of the power of the air and because he can transform to be an angel of light, he can take on the form of leviathan in the marine world and behemoth on the land. The dominion he exerts on planet earth was stolen from Adam; he is a thief and Jesus came just to defeat him with his evil cohort. Jesus defeated and disarmed all of them in their copied ranks and their villainous strategy according to Colossians 2:15,

Having disarmed principalities and powers, He made a public spectacle of them, triumphing over them in it.

Hallelujah! These fallen angels are not demons as commonly mistaken by many. Like I mentioned earlier, I discovered through personal revelation that demons are not the same as fallen angels. The fallen angels manifest as princes of darkness or dark princes (principality), they love to control thrones and for every physical or political title you see in the physical realm, there is a spiritual counterpart. Every title, regardless of who bears it, has a principality controlling it from the spiritual hierarchy. If the land or territory is full of intercessors, then the ruling prince will be a godly angel like Michael in Daniel 10 (a prince of God's people). But if the land or territory is full of godless men, then the ruling prince will be evil or a fallen angel. They were made to rule territories. They love big title and also love to control rulers and kings. The bigger the title, the more likely there is a spirit prince involved over the territory.

> **Ephesians 6:12** - *For we do not wrestle against flesh and blood, but against principalities, against powers, against the rulers of the darkness of this age, against spiritual hosts of wickedness in the heavenly places.*

Our consolation lies in the fact that we have a greater and better hierarchy! An highly organized army of the Lord that was cheaply copied by the adversary.

> **Ephesians 1:20-21** - *Which He worked in Christ when He raised Him from the dead and seated Him at His right hand in the heavenly places, far above all principality and power and might and dominion, and every name that is named, not only in this age but also in that which is to come.*

And Ephesian 2:6 says we are seated with Christ above all of them. We belong to the winning side with more troops and a formidable army that has completely won the battle.

# MANIFESTATION OF EVIL PRINCES

A dark prince (principality) is a fallen angel who rules over regions and bears the alternate title in the spirit realm for any big title, and controls that physical throne regardless of who bears it on the earth. Principalities manifest through great kings like Herod, Pharaoh, Caesar and evil personalities like Haman and Jezebel. They also tend to take charge over eras of human civilization. This is why the Bible tells us to pray for our leaders in 1 Timothy 2:1-2,

> *Therefore I exhort first of all that supplications, prayers, intercessions, and giving of thanks be made for all men, ² for kings and all who are in authority, that we may lead a quiet and peaceable life in all godliness and reverence.*

When you pray for your land and the leaders, you will be engaging heavenly princes like Angel Michael to defend and govern such territories. When Daniel was fasting and praying for 21 days, he was actually waging war against the host of darkness and his prayer brought the chief prince or archangel Michael into the scene. Note that the Bible referred to both the evil angel and the godly angel as princes in Daniel 10: 12-13,

> *Then he said to me, "Do not fear, Daniel, for from the first day that you set your heart to understand, and to humble yourself before your God, your words were heard; and I have come because of your words. ¹³ But the prince of the kingdom of Persia withstood me twenty-one days; and behold, Michael, one of the chief princes, came to help me, for I had been left alone there with the kings of Persia.*

**Note**: When dealing with Satan and fallen angels you resist and rebuke them in the name of Jesus. You don't cast them out or bind them like demons. See examples from Scriptures:

> **James 4:7** - *Therefore submit to God. Resist the devil and he will flee from you.*

> **1 Peter 5:8-9** - *Be sober, be vigilant; because your adversary the devil walks about like a roaring lion, seeking whom he may devour. ⁹ Resist him, steadfast in the faith, knowing that the same sufferings are experienced by your brotherhood in the world.*

> **Jude 1:9** - *Yet Michael the archangel, in contending with the devil, when he disputed about the body of Moses, dared not bring against him a reviling accusation, but said, "The Lord rebuke you!"*

Let us take a look at an example of an evil prince and the spiritual counterpart from the scriptures in Ezekiel 28:

## THE PRINCE OF TYRE

> *The word of the Lord came again to me, saying, ² Son of man, say to the prince of Tyre, Thus says the Lord God: Because your heart is lifted up and you have said and thought, I am a god, I sit in the seat of the gods, in the heart of the seas; yet you are only man [weak, feeble, made of earth] and not God, though you imagine yourself to be almost more than mortal with your mind as the mind of God; ³ Indeed, you are [imagining yourself] wiser than Daniel; there is no secret [you think] that is hidden from you; ⁴ With your own wisdom and with your own understanding you have gotten you riches and power and have brought gold and silver into your treasuries; ⁵ By your great*

*wisdom and by your traffic you have increased your riches and power, and your heart is proud and lifted up because of your wealth;* <sup>6</sup> *Therefore thus says the Lord God: Because you have imagined your mind as the mind of God [having thoughts and purposes suitable only to God Himself],* <sup>7</sup> *Behold therefore, I am bringing strangers upon you, the most terrible of the nations, and they shall draw their swords against the beauty of your wisdom [O Tyre], and they shall defile your splendor.* <sup>8</sup> *They shall bring you down to the pit [of destruction] and you shall die the [many] deaths of all the Tyrians that are slain in the heart of the seas.* <sup>9</sup> *Will you still say, I am a god, before him who slays you? But you are only a man [made of earth] and no god in the hand of him who wounds and profanes you.* <sup>10</sup> *You shall die the death of the uncircumcised by the hand of strangers, for I have spoken it, says the Lord God. (AMP)*

The prince of Tyre above looks like a physical or human king who was controlled by the spiritual counterpart called the king of Tyre below. If you read the description properly, you will discover that it is describing none other than the fallen cherub Lucifer himself.

## THE KING OF TYRE

*Moreover, the word of the Lord came to me, saying,* <sup>12</sup> *Son of man, take up a lamentation over the king of Tyre and say to him, Thus says the Lord God: You are the full measure and pattern of exactness [giving the finishing touch to all that constitutes completeness], full of wisdom and perfect in beauty.* <sup>13</sup> *You were in Eden, the garden of God; every precious stone was your covering, the carnelian, topaz, jasper, chrysolite, beryl, onyx, sapphire, carbuncle, and emerald; and your settings and your sockets and engravings were wrought in gold. On the day that you were created they were prepared. ¹⁴ You were the anointed cherub that covers with overshadowing [wings], and I set you so. You were upon the holy mountain of God; you walked up and down in the midst of the stones of fire [like the paved work of gleaming sapphire stone upon which the God of Israel walked on Mount Sinai].¹⁵ You were blameless in your ways from the day you were created until iniquity and guilt were found in you. ¹⁶ Through the abundance of your commerce you were filled with lawlessness and violence, and you sinned; therefore I cast you out as a profane thing from the mountain of God and the guardian cherub drove you out from the midst of the stones of fire. ¹⁷ Your heart was proud and lifted up because of your beauty; you corrupted your wisdom for the sake of your splendor. I cast you to the ground; I lay you before kings, that they might gaze at you. ¹⁸ You have profaned your sanctuaries by the multitude of your iniquities and the enormity of your guilt, by the unrighteousness of your trade. Therefore I have brought forth a fire from your midst; it has consumed you, and I have reduced you to ashes upon the earth in the sight of all who looked at you. ¹⁹ All who know you among the people are astonished and appalled at you; you have come to a horrible end and shall never return to being.*

We can see some other evil personalities or principalities below:

## HEROD

Who is Herod? He is the wicked king who is always looking to behead God's anointed one. He requested for the head of baby Jesus and was dealt with in Matthew 2:16,19:

*Then Herod, when he saw that he was deceived by the wise men, was exceedingly angry; and he sent forth and put to death all*

*the male children who were in Bethlehem and in all its districts,
from two years old and under, according to the time which he
had determined from the wise men. Now when Herod was dead,
behold, an angel of the Lord appeared in a dream to Joseph in
Egypt.*

He is the same king who requested for the head of the
greatest prophet who ever lived – John the Baptist in Matthew
14:3,5-6,8,10:

*For Herod had laid hold of John and bound him, and put him
in prison for the sake of Herodias, his brother Philip's wife.
And although he wanted to put him to death, he feared the
multitude, because they counted him as a prophet. But when
Herod's birthday was celebrated, the daughter of Herodias
danced before them and pleased Herod. So she, having been
prompted by her mother, said, "Give me John the Baptist's head
here on a platter." So he sent and had John beheaded in prison.*

## HEROD AND JOHN SHARED HISTORY

Biblical prophecy shows that John the Baptist will return in
the spirit and power of Elijah so the evil personality who
could not get Elijah's head in the past revisited him because
of Luke 1:17 He will also go before Him(Messiah) in the
spirit and power of Elijah, 'to turn the hearts of the fathers
to the children,' and the disobedient to the wisdom of the
just, to make ready a people prepared for the Lord.''. Elijah
escaped death from Jezebel but Herodias retaliated in John
the Baptist. Remember her threat in 1 Kings 19:1-2,

*And Ahab told Jezebel all that Elijah had done, also how he
had executed all the prophets with the sword. Then Jezebel sent*

*a messenger to Elijah, saying, "So let the gods do to me, and more also, if I do not make your life as the life of one of them by tomorrow about this time."*

The kingdom of darkness has a habit of revisiting battles and can be very vengeful. The only reason why this evil personality could win this time around was because of the offense in John the Baptist (Matthew 11:2-6). Beware of offences; they expose you to the onslaught of the wicked one.

## PHARAOH

Who is Pharaoh? Pharaoh is a prince of darkness that afflicts God's chosen people. It is the evil power that will go to any extent to limit the work of one's hands and is threatened by great destinies. This is the force that exchanges work and blessings for profitless hard labor and toiling.

It is the power that keeps one's head down instead of allowing God's divine lifting to take place; it turns plenty to scarcity and exchanges dignity for shame. This power has subverted many destinies and sentenced many to untimely graves. This is the evil prince that turns many kings and priests to earthly slaves. He makes life very bitter and has a personal vendetta against the male seed. This power negotiates how far many can go in life. It even holds many generations to ransom in slavery. This is the power behind "working like an elephant but eating like an ant". He will inflict pain and afflict people with hard bondage. It is the force that will militate against your will to serve God and will not allow you to openly profess your faith. We see a replica of this in the book of Exodus. There we can see the afflictions Pharaoh placed on the Israelites.

Pharaoh has swallowed up many generations in abject poverty and threatened many champions to silence. This is a very stubborn force that refuses to give in easily despite seeing the finger of God. He is a bloodthirsty killer and a diabolical taskmaster.

Pharaoh is merciless and ruthless and must be treated in the same ruthless manner. He is a master negotiator and an unrepentant adversary that will still come after you despite seeming victory. Pharaoh must be completely discomfited and swallowed up in the Red Sea! Today, the Red Sea that drowns Pharaoh is the blood of Jesus.

**REFLECTION**:
*Holy Ghost, show me the secrets of spiritual warfare and give me an understanding of the authority over principalities and powers that I have in Christ Jesus.*

# 5

## Demons

### THE ORIGIN OF DEMONIC AFFLICTION

WHAT ARE DEMONS and where do they come from? God did not create demons! They are abnormal – an aberration that originated from the devil himself. I did a diligent search through the scriptures about where they originated from but found almost nothing. It was as if the Bible was very silent about where they came from and they just sprung up like trees without roots in the New Testament. If you look closely at the life and ministry of Jesus Christ our Savior on the earth, you will observe that He was very busy casting out these unclean spirits or demons. His ministry was filled with dealing with the archenemy (the devil) and his demonic cohort also known as "unclean spirits, demons, devils or foul spirits".

> **Act 10:38** - *How God anointed Jesus of Nazareth with the Holy Spirit and with power, who went about doing good and healing all who were oppressed by the devil, for God was with Him.*

These demonic spirits exist in an organized hierarchy that was copied from the Kingdom of our heavenly Father. They even revered Christ and knew who He was the minute they set eyes on Him. This was also very common and recorded in the lives of the apostles throughout the Acts of the Apostles. Jesus was binding these foul spirits and setting people free. The mandate that the Lord committed into our hands has this instruction as well,

> **Mark 16:17-18** - *And these signs will follow those who believe: In My name they will cast out demons; they will speak with new tongues;* [18] *they will take up serpents; and if they drink anything deadly, it will by no means hurt them; they will lay hands on the sick, and they will recover."*

Satan is different from fallen angels and fallen angels are different from the demons. As much as possible, I will try to explain the difference between them as revealed to me in the place of studying the word of God and praying. If you are in doubt just go back to the Teacher (the Holy Spirit) to teach you. Ask Him and He will show you great and mighty things you do not know (Jeremiah 33:3). Please do not take my words as the final authority but seek the truth from the Lord yourself. The Bible says you must test all spirits, prove all things and hold fast to that which is true.

> **1 Thessalonians 5:21** - *Test all things; hold fast what is good.*

> **1 John 4:1** - *Beloved, do not believe every spirit, but test the spirits, whether they are of God because many false prophets have gone out into the world.*

No matter who is preaching or teaching you the Word, make sure you confirm it through the scriptures and the Author Himself – the Holy Spirit.

Demons are described in the Bible as foul spirits or unclean spirits. They usually crave to indwell or possess human beings. If they cannot find a dwelling in any human, they will beg to inhabit or possess an animal or even a tree or graven image; that is what makes such items or things enchanted. I am of the conviction that demons are the offspring of the fallen angels who mated with the women in Genesis 6:1-8. The New King James version renders it this way,

> Now it came to pass, when men began to multiply on the face of the earth, and daughters were born to them, ² that the sons of God saw the daughters of men, that they were beautiful; and they took wives for themselves of all whom they chose. ³ And the LORD said, "My Spirit shall not strive with man forever, for he is indeed flesh; yet his days shall be one hundred and twenty years." ⁴ There were giants on the earth in those days, and also afterward, when the sons of God came in to the daughters of men and they bore children to them. Those were the mighty men who were of old, men of renown. ⁵ Then the LORD saw that the wickedness of man was great in the earth, and that every intent of the thoughts of his heart was only evil continually. ⁶ And the LORD was sorry that He had made man on the earth, and He was grieved in His heart. ⁷ So the LORD said, "I will destroy man whom I have created from the face of the earth, both man and beast, creeping thing and birds of the air, for I am sorry that I have made them." ⁸ But Noah found grace in the eyes of the LORD.

I know someone may be wondering how the "sons of God" in the above verses of scripture meant fallen angels but you will need to read other Bible translations to see this. One version of this scripture that I would like to share is the Living Bible version. Here we see that the "sons of God" meant angels or spirit beings.

**Genesis 6:1-6** - *Now a population explosion took place upon the earth. It was at this time that beings from the spirit world looked upon the beautiful earth women and took any they desired to be their wives. ³ Then Jehovah said, "My Spirit must not forever be disgraced in man, wholly evil as he is. I will give him 120 years to mend his ways." ⁴ In those days, and even afterwards, when the evil beings from the spirit world were sexually involved with human women, their children became giants, of whom so many legends are told. ⁵ When the Lord God saw the extent of human wickedness, and that the trend and direction of men's lives were only towards evil, ⁶ he was sorry he had made them. It broke his heart. (TLB)*

God wiped out the tainted human race corrupted by the evil combination of fall angels and earthly women (human). He wiped them out in the flood. He had been watching a particular family that refused to be tainted by this evil blood and it was the generation of His friend Enoch. Noah was Enoch's grandson and the Bible records that despite the extent of man's depravity, God's grace still came into play. Noah and his entire household found grace, just like you and I have found the grace of God through salvation in the blood of Jesus Christ.

After everyone died in Genesis 7, I believe that the spirits of the fallen angels went to the place of punishment created for them according to Jude 1:6, and the spirits of the human mothers as well as all other human beings on earth at that time went to the holding place for human spirits after death – which is Hades. But these "aberrations" also known as "unclean spirits" became disembodied spirits that we now call demons. They were wicked then and are still wicked now with a bloodthirsty vendetta to destroy the human race. They love to indwell human bodies first because they were partly humans and also because they need a physical body to carry out all their wicked depravity. For example, a demon of sexual immorality or addiction needs a body to carry out such desires. I do not believe that the fallen angels are demons because the Bible records that angels excel in strength and are usually mighty beings – that was just how the Creator made them. He made them that way so that they could fulfill their purpose to serve Him and serve the heirs of salvation.

If you look through the scriptures, you will agree with me that they were huge and sometimes super-sized according to the different visions of Ezekiel, Isaiah, Daniel and the apostles. They appeared with great aura of light and such powerful presence that many of the patriarchs passed out in awe when they behold them. Imagine these super-sized beings trying to fit into the small frame of a human. Remember that fallen angels are still angels but they are fallen. They would prefer to lord it over nations and territories than just be limited to a little body. The King of Tyre and the prince of Tyre in Isaiah 18 are typical of the description of fallen angels or evil personalities. They will rather be principalities like the prince of Persia in Daniel 10 than a little imp possessing someone.

When the teacher was speaking of death (i.e. man's final departure from the earthy realm in Ecclesiastes 12:6-7), He spoke of the silver cord.

> *Remember your Creator before the silver cord is loosed,*
> *Or the golden bowl is broken,*
> *Or the pitcher shattered at the fountain,*
> *Or the wheel broken at the well.*
> *[7] Then the dust will return to the earth as it was,*
> *And the spirit will return to God who gave it.*

The silver cord is the breath of life that sustains man; when it is broken, man ceases to be. I really want to emphasize that God made man so when man dies, his spirit goes back to God. But God did not make the aberrations created by the fallen angels and the women of Genesis 6. They are not God's creation but are deviations from the original human species. This is why they turned out to be giants and were called men of great stature or men of renown. They combined the super-strength of their fathers with the human looks of their mothers but their thoughts were evil continually and this was what grieved God in Genesis 6:1. God was grieved because of the mutants formed by this unholy union. That was why He wiped out the tainted and corrupted human race.

> **Genesis 6:9-11** - *This is the genealogy of Noah. Noah was a just man, perfect in his generations. Noah walked with God. ¹⁰ And Noah begot three sons: Shem, Ham, and Japheth. ¹¹ The earth also was corrupt before God, and the earth was filled with violence. ¹² So God looked upon the earth, and indeed it was corrupt; for all flesh had corrupted their way on the earth.*

But Noah found grace in the eyes of God because his family was the purest or closest to the original as God made it. He preserved Noah's family to repopulate the earth after the flood. God had been watching this lineage for a while – remember Enoch his grandfather and his father Methuselah? God was looking at the people who didn't marry into the tainted race. He gave man another chance because He loves man above all of His creation. Every living creature that was not in the ark with Noah and his household died. The entire creation lost its mind and there was no more sense of right or wrong. God had to divinely intervene and deal with the extreme depravity of mankind but because He still loved man so much, He chose not to completely wipe out the human race because of the evil angels. He offered grace to Noah and that is the same grace that was revealed to us through Christ Jesus.

> **Genesis 8:22-24** - *All in whose nostrils was the breath of the spirit of life, all that was on the dry land, died. [23] So He destroyed all living things which were on the face of the ground: both man and cattle, creeping thing and bird of the air. They were destroyed from the earth. Only Noah and those who were with him in the ark remained alive. [24] And the waters prevailed on the earth one hundred and fifty days.*

The human spirits went back to God who made them (Ecclesiastes 12:7). The fallen angels went into eternal damnation in the dungeons reserved for them till the final judgment day according to Jude 1:6,

And the angels who did not keep their proper domain, but left their own abode, He has reserved in everlasting chains under darkness for the judgment of the great day.

My question to you now is where do you think the spirit of the offspring of the fallen angels and women went? Unlike their human mothers, they couldn't go to God because He did not make them. They did not go to the dungeons with their fallen angel fathers. So they became hovering spirits on the face of the earth – millions and billions of them.

They became man's enemy forever! They will never serve the Lord God and cannot repent of their sins because no provision is made to accommodate them. Hell and the Lake of fire is actually their final destination after the great judgment day. The Bible says we will judge angels – I believe we will! These foul spirits have dwelled in living bodies before they died. They had real cravings and indulgences before the bodies died. They had super-powers and the Bible records that they were giants as tall as 9 feet or more.

Every book I have read from people who have seen a physical manifestation of demonic spirits describes them as tall beings. They need a body to carry out their cravings and depravity. They will do anything to possess a living human and when they are expelled out of a particular body, they will go out and bring seven stronger demons back into that body. Some of them are demons of addictions – sexual, drug, food and the like. Some manifest through sexual perversion such as pedophilia, homosexuality and lesbianism. Many demonic spirits manifest as bloodthirsty serial killers and cannibals.

Another set of demonic spirits manifest as spirits of affliction of the body or mind of human beings – they cause sickness and bring insanity. Some of these demons manifest through witchcraft and sorcery. Their mission is to take over the life of the individual possessed by the demons like the devil's mission to kill, steal and destroy. They create evil habitation in human bodies in the form of tumors and cancers. They can operate as deaf and dumb spirits. Some of them are offspring of angels of death and are obsessed with suicidal ideas and enjoy carrying out creepy forms of death.

Demons create yokes and help populate satanic prisons. Jesus said clearly that this kind (demons) do not go out except through fasting and prayer (Matthew 17:21). The mandate of every believer is to send out these demons. They are sometimes referred to as the strongman (see Matthew 12:29). Your mandate as a believer is to cast them out and set people free from their bondage according to Mark 16:17-18,

> *And these signs will follow those who believe: In My name they will cast out demons; they will speak with new tongues; ¹⁸ they will take up serpents; and if they drink anything deadly, it will by no means hurt them; they will lay hands on the sick, and they will recover."*

**REFLECTION:**
***Father Lord, help me to demonstrate the authority given to me by Christ Jesus over demons, principalities and powers. I receive the anointing to set the captives free like my Jesus.***

# 6

# *The Chosen Fast*

## A PRESCRIPTION FOR DELIVERANCE

THERE IS A CHOSEN FAST that breaks the yoke of the enemy and it can be seen in Isaiah 58:6-9. This fast was what Jesus was referring to when His disciples could not expel the demon afflicting a man's son in Matthew 17:21. He said this kind (of demonic spirit) goes not out except by fasting and prayer. When you observe fasting as prescribed by the Lord (i.e. when you completely strip the soul bare of every fleshly tendencies and the spirit is empowered to hear from God directly), yokes will be destroyed. When you combine this fast with aggressive prayers and high praises, you will have the results that all the patriarchs of old had. You will command the same results that Jesus commanded – Jesus fasted and prayed through all the watches (please refer to Day 2 of my book *The Chosen Fast* for a detailed explanation of the prayer watches). For you to defeat the enemy cheaply, you must do what Jesus did.

See the scripture in Isaiah 58:

> *Is this not the fast that I have chosen:*
> *To loose the bonds of wickedness,*
> *To undo the heavy burdens,*

*To let the oppressed go free,*
*And that you break every yoke?*
*⁷ Is it not to share your bread with the hungry,*
*And that you bring to your house the poor who are cast out;*
*When you see the naked, that you cover him,*
*And not hide yourself from your own flesh?*
*⁸ Then your light shall break forth like the morning,*
*Your healing shall spring forth speedily,*
*And your righteousness shall go before you;*
*The glory of the LORD shall be your rear guard.*
*⁹ Then you shall call, and the LORD will answer;*
*You shall cry, and He will say, 'Here I am.'*

## WHAT IS FASTING?

Fasting is abstaining from food and water for a season. It is not to get your wish list granted or to bribe God for your needs to be met. Fasting does not change God's mind, fasting changes you! You subdue the flesh in a fast and your spirit (the true you) comes alive. It silences the voice of the flesh so that the voice of the Spirit is amplified. It intensifies our ability to perceive the manifest presence of God.

Fasting is primarily an act of willing abstinence or reduction from certain or all food, drink, or both, for a period of time. An absolute fast is normally defined as abstinence from all food and liquid for a defined period, usually a single day (24 hours), or several days. Other fasts may be only partially restrictive, limiting particular foods or substances. The fast may also be intermittent in nature. Fasting practices may preclude sexual intercourse and other activities as well as food.

**1 Corinthians 7:3-5** - *Let the husband render to his wife the affection due her, and likewise also the wife to her husband.*

*⁴ The wife does not have authority over her own body, but the husband does. And likewise the husband does not have authority over his own body, but the wife does. ⁵ Do not deprive one another except with consent for a time, that you may give yourselves to fasting and prayer; and come together again so that Satan does not tempt you because of your lack of self-control.*

There are some things that will not yield or leave without fasting accompanied with prayer and expelling demons is one of them. Jesus, addressing His disciples when they could not heal a boy that was troubled by demonic spirits, said in Matthew 17:21,

*However, this kind does not go out except by prayer and fasting.*

In order for you to address some satanic afflictions and destroy the works of the flesh, you must be willing to fast and pray. Abstaining from food as a religious obligation without heartfelt prayers is tantamount to hunger strike – it is not productive and will yield no tangible result. In fact, it is destructive and can impact your physical health negatively. There is an acceptable fast according to scriptures and my prayer is that by the time you are through with this book, you would have mastered spiritual warfare empowered by fasting. This chosen fast sets people free from satanic bondages and demonic oppressions. It removes heavy burdens, lets the oppressed go free and breaks every yoke of the enemy.

Deliverance is confirmed in Isaiah 61:1-3. The spirit of heaviness or depression is mentioned in verse 3 and how to heal a broken heart is stated clearly in verse 1. It sets at liberty those who are locked up in spiritual and physical prisons. The only antidote for sorrow or depression is **intentional praise**. Demons cannot stand the manifest presence of God and praise brings down God's presence. No wonder David kept Saul's tormentors at bay whenever he praised God. The scriptures in Isaiah 61 calls it the garment of praise. I would also mention that demons flee from the oil of joy or gladness – both the physical oil (anointing oil) and the spiritual oil (Holy Spirit). The oil is mentioned in verse 3 and it must remain ever fresh and not stale.

> *The Spirit of the Lord GOD is upon Me,*
> *Because the LORD has anointed Me*
> *To preach good tidings to the poor;*
> *He has sent Me to heal the brokenhearted,*
> *To proclaim liberty to the captives,*
> *And the opening of the prison to those who are bound;*
> *² To proclaim the acceptable year of the LORD,*
> *And the day of vengeance of our God;*
> *To comfort all who mourn,*
> *³ To console those who mourn in Zion,*
> *To give them beauty for ashes,*
> *The oil of joy for mourning,*
> *The garment of praise for the spirit of heaviness;*
> *That they may be called trees of righteousness,*
> *The planting of the LORD, that He may be glorified.*

The Psalmist referred to it in Psalms 92:10 as fresh oil that exalts. I like the King James Version best because it is easy to picture the horn of a unicorn.

> *But my horn shalt thou exalt like the horn of an unicorn: I shall*
> *be anointed with fresh oil. (KJV)*

It was also mentioned in the very popular Psalm 23 (verse 5); the entire chapter was very literal for me during those panic attacks. I applied the anointing oil on myself and my entire household many times and this yielded immediate relief.

*⁵ You prepare a table before me in the presence of my enemies; You anoint my head with oil; My cup runs over.*

We know from the Word of God that anointing oil breaks the yoke. Anointing oil is very crucial to breaking demonic oppression. Isaiah 10:27 says,

*And It shall come to pass in that day That his burden will be taken away from your shoulder, And his **yoke** from your neck, And the **yoke** will be destroyed because of the **anointing** oil.*

And this is restated in the book of James 5:14-15 that you can use the physical oil to pray for the sick to receive healing,

*Is anyone among you sick? Let him call for the elders of the church, and let them pray over him, anointing him with oil in the name of the Lord. ¹⁵ And the prayer of faith will save the sick, and the Lord will raise him up. And if he has committed sins, he will be forgiven.*

There is an exceeding great mystery in the oil that the logical mind or theological philosophy cannot explain but it has worked for me. You may be asking as you read this book, "Where will I get the anointing oil?" It is very simple to get one. You can use any cooking oil you have at home or buy some from the grocery store and pray over it. Preferably olive oil that is most easily available as stated in scriptures.

**Exodus 30:22-30** - *Moreover the* LORD *spoke to Moses, saying: ²³ "Also take for yourself quality spices—five hundred shekels of liquid myrrh, half as much sweet-smelling cinnamon*

*(two hundred and fifty shekels), two hundred and fifty shekels of sweet-smelling cane, <sup>24</sup> five hundred shekels of cassia, according to the shekel of the sanctuary, and a hin of olive oil. <sup>25</sup> And you shall make from these a holy anointing oil, an ointment compounded according to the art of the perfumer. It shall be a holy anointing oil. <sup>26</sup> With it you shall anoint the tabernacle of meeting and the ark of the Testimony; <sup>27</sup> the table and all its utensils, the lampstand and its utensils, and the altar of incense; <sup>28</sup> the altar of burnt offering with all its utensils, and the laver and its base. <sup>29</sup> You shall consecrate them, that they may be most holy; whatever touches them must be holy. <sup>30</sup> And you shall anoint Aaron and his sons, and consecrate them, that they may minister to Me as priests."*

Are you wondering if you are qualified to pray over the oil? As a believer, yes you can. First, the Lord has called you as kings and priests unto Himself and He has made you holy and set apart for His use when you gave your life to Christ. You are the righteousness of God in Christ Jesus! Therefore, you are qualified. There are intensities and degrees of the anointing.

For example, Jesus had the spirit without measure and certain people have grown in their walk with God like Moses, Paul and Peter whose shadows could heal the sick and whose handkerchiefs could raise the dead (Acts 19:12, Acts 5:15). It is wise to get more fire from such anointed individuals when you come in contact with them in-person or through their ministrations. I keep fortifying my anointing oil and I never lack one at any time.

As a born-again child of God, you have the same spirit that was in Peter, Paul, and most importantly, our Lord Jesus Christ. You can cast out demons and you can break satanic yokes because they have been placed under your feet.

> **Luke 10:19** - *Behold, I give you the authority to trample on serpents and scorpions, and over all the power of the enemy, and nothing shall by any means hurt you.*

**REFLECTION**:
***Father Lord, I thank you for the power you have endowed me with, to demolish the habitations of cruelty through the blood of Jesus Christ our Lord!***

# 7
# *Dressed for Battle*

FOR US TO BE BATTLE-READY, we must be properly dressed in the full military outfit appropriate for spiritual warfare. Every soldier enlisted in a physical army must be fitted in the right gear or outfit to make him battle-ready. In the military, it is a must for you to wear the appropriate outfit for the battlefield. The Bible says no man enlisted in the army entangles himself with civilian matters (2 Timothy 2:4). You cannot wear a ceremonial gown of a bishop or a pope when going to the war-fields of Afghanistan; it will trip you up and get in your way. Just as in the physical, where you need a physical uniform or battle-gear to put on for battle, so also in the spirit realm, you must be dressed in the appropriate outfit. Jesus is the Captain of the angelic host and He is the One leading us in battle. We are supposed to follow His example completely;

The Lord is a Man of War and His battle gear is described in Isaiah 59:16-17,

> *He saw that there was no man,*
> *And wondered that there was no intercessor;*
> *Therefore His own arm brought salvation for Him;*
> *And His own righteousness, it sustained Him.*

*<sup>17</sup> For He put on righteousness as a breastplate,*
*And a helmet of salvation on His head;*
*He put on the garments of vengeance for clothing,*
*And was clad with zeal as a cloak.*

The same outfit is set apart for every believer enlisted in the Lord's army. Ephesians 6:10-18 talks about getting equipped for spiritual warfare. It is clear from this scripture that we are not fighting against flesh and blood (human adversaries) but against persons without bodies (spiritual beings) as stated in the Living Bible translation below:

*For we are not fighting against people made of flesh and blood, but against persons without bodies—the evil rulers of the unseen world, those mighty satanic beings and great evil princes of darkness who rule this world; and against huge numbers of wicked spirits in the spirit world.*

The rendition is a little different in the New King James version but I added it for emphasis so we can easily see all the seven weapons available to us as believers to defeat the devil and his cohorts. Ephesians 6:10-18 describes the whole armor of God; it was similar to the military outfit of a Roman soldier in the days of Paul the Apostle who wrote this letter to the Christians at Ephesus:

*Finally, my brethren, be strong in the Lord and in the power of His might. <sup>11</sup> Put on the whole armor of God, that you may be able to stand against the wiles of the devil. <sup>12</sup> For we do not wrestle against flesh and blood, but against principalities, against powers, against the rulers of the darkness of this age, against spiritual hosts of wickedness in the heavenly places. <sup>13</sup> Therefore take up the whole armor of God, that you may be able to withstand in the* *evil day, and having done all, to stand. <sup>14</sup> Stand therefore, having girded your waist with truth, having put on the breastplate of righteousness, <sup>15</sup> and having shod your feet with the preparation of the gospel of peace; <sup>16</sup> above all, taking the shield of faith with which you will be able to quench all the fiery darts of the wicked one. <sup>17</sup> And take the helmet of salvation, and the sword of the Spirit, which is the word of God; <sup>18</sup> praying always with all prayer and supplication in the Spirit, being watchful to this end with all perseverance and supplication for all the saints.*

## THE FULL GEAR – THE WHOLE ARMOR OF GOD FROM HEAD TO TOE:

**1. Helmet of Salvation:** Every soldier in this army must be born-again to be able to stand in this battle. At salvation, whether you realize it or not, you have been enlisted into the ongoing battle despite the fact that it started before you were even born. The minute you became born-again, the sign was clearly seen on your forehead in the spirit realm saying, TOUCH NOT! SAVED! REDEEMED BY THE BLOOD! HOLY NATION! ROYAL PRIESTHOOD! PECULIAR!

When you examine the scriptures in Exodus 28:38 and Revelation 22:4, you will see that there is always an inscription on the forehead showing the mark of redemption forever. This helmet also protects your head (brain) or your mind. It is important to have your mind protected from the onslaught of the enemy because the mind is a battlefield on its own.

The truth is that before salvation, you were of no consequence to the adversary. To him, you were just a clueless bystander but the danger was that you could have been a casualty of war. However, the moment you acknowledged Jesus as Lord and

Savior, you were automatically drafted into the winning camp – the Kingdom of His marvelous light.

> **1 Peter 2:9-10** - *But you are a chosen generation, a royal priesthood, a holy nation, His own special people, that you may proclaim the praises of Him who called you out of darkness into His marvelous light; ¹⁰ who once were not a people but are now the people of God, who had not obtained mercy but now have obtained mercy.*

**2. Breastplate of Righteousness:** This piece of the battle gear was also worn by our Lord Jesus Christ (Isaiah 59:17) and the priest in the Old Testament (Exodus 28: 29-30). It protects the heart or the seat of your emotions, out of which comes the issues of life. The breastplate of righteousness gives you the right standing you need to approach the throne of grace according to Hebrews 4:16. The righteousness you now have has nothing to do with your past or your ability to fulfill the law. The precious blood of Jesus obtained this righteousness and it is purely ours by grace. The enemy we face is a very legalistic devil called the accuser of the brethren, he lives to condemn through the law and so the breastplate of righteousness is necessary to destroy the condemnation powered by the conscience. This voice has been completely silenced by what the Son of God did for us on the cross according to:

> **Romans 8:1-4** - *There is therefore now no condemnation to those who are in Christ Jesus, who do not walk according to the flesh, but according to the Spirit. ² For the law of the Spirit of life in Christ Jesus has made me free from the law of sin and death. ³ For what the law could not do in that it was weak through the flesh, God did by sending His own Son in the likeness of sinful flesh, on account of sin: He condemned sin in the flesh, ⁴ that the*

*righteous requirement of the law might be fulfilled in us who do not walk according to the flesh but according to the Spirit.*

**3. The Belt of Truth:** The belt wraps around the waistline and it is meant to protect your loin and colon area. The belt or girdle will keep the skirt of the Roman soldier from falling and it also holds all the other weapons in place just like the uniform of a modern day military man. The belt of truth represents truth in the inward parts according to the Psalmist in Psalms 51:6,

*Behold, You desire truth in the inward parts, And in the hidden part You will make me to know wisdom.*

Having a consecrated sexuality is crucial in your walk with the Lord. The Bible says that every sin is done outside the body but sexual sin is done against one's body; it exposes you and burns your guts (Proverbs 7:23); it strikes the liver and burns open spiritual covering (Proverbs 6:27). When God called Abraham in Genesis 17, He demanded circumcision from His generation. The same happened when Moses was going to fulfill His assignment of bringing God's people out of bondage – his sons had to be consecrated so that they don't fall into trouble with the idolatrous lifestyle of Egypt. God is calling every soldier to complete consecration in the loins because the devil caused many champions to trip through this avenue and they were written in scripture for our example e.g. David, Solomon and Samson just to name a few.

There is also a need to protect the belly, which holds your emotions as well. Anxiety, fear, bitterness are all emotions you can feel in your guts and medical studies show that these emotions elicit negative reactions or hormones in the body.

Colon cancer, ulcers and irritable bowel syndromes are closely related to unforgiveness, anxiety and bitterness. Ephesians 4:25-27 addresses truth, anger and forgiving quickly:

> *Therefore, putting away lying, "Let each one of you speak truth with his neighbor," for we are members of one another. [26] "Be angry, and do not sin": do not let the sun go down on your wrath, [27] nor give place to the devil.*

Further down that scripture, you will also see that carrying unforgiveness or anger around exposes you to spiritual warfare. All these negative emotions amplifies the flesh or sin nature and grieves the Holy Spirit, thus diminishing His power at work in your life.

> **Ephesians 4:30-32** - *And do not grieve the Holy Spirit of God, by whom you were sealed for the day of redemption. [31] Let all bitterness, wrath, anger, clamor, and evil speaking be put away from you, with all malice. [32] And be kind to one another, tenderhearted, forgiving one another, even as God in Christ forgave you.*

**4. Shield of Faith:** This piece of spiritual armory provides powerful covering according to Ephesians 6:16,

> *Above all, taking the shield of faith with which you will be able to quench all the fiery darts of the wicked one.*

The shield of faith protects the vital organs on your left side (especially your heart) from being pierced by the fiery darts of the enemy. The shield is a powerful protection against enchantments and divinations as well as the scourge of the tongue (Job 5:21). The enemy has a way of defaming one's character through the evil device of the tongue and it can bring discouragement. When Joshua was setting out as the new leader of God's people in Joshua 1, God kept telling Joshua to be strong and of good courage and not be afraid, dismayed or discouraged. When David was going to set out after the enemy to recover his family member and possessions in 1 Samuel 30, he encouraged himself in the Lord. Faith is an important ingredient in spiritual warfare and the enemy will rather torment with fear and timidity but God said he has not given us the spirit of fear but of love, power and a sound mind. You need a sound mind to fight a battle. The tactics of the enemy is to put fear and discouragement in you.

The strategy of discouragement is for the believer to lose the courage or faith needed to fight and overcome in spiritual warfare.

> **1 John 5:4** - *For whatever is born of God overcomes the world. And this is the* **victory** *that has overcome the world even our* **faith**.

The Bible says in 1 Peter 5:8,

> *Be sober, be vigilant; because your adversary the devil walks about like a roaring lion, seeking whom he may devour.* [9] **Resist** *him, steadfast in the* **faith**, *knowing that the same sufferings are experienced by your brotherhood in the world.* [10] *But may the God of all grace, who called us to His eternal glory by Christ Jesus, after you have suffered a while, perfect, establish, strengthen, and settle you.*

**5. Sword of the Spirit:** The sword of the spirit is the Word of God. Every believer must possess the mouth described in

Luke 21:15 (a mouth and a wisdom which the adversary cannot resist nor gainsay) because the Word of God is a double-edged sword in your mouth.

> **Hebrews 4:12** - *For the word of God is living and powerful, and sharper than any two-edged sword, piercing even to the division of soul and spirit, and of joints and marrow, and is a discerner of the thoughts and intents of the heart.*

A closed mouth is a closed destiny and an unopened Bible is a redundant weapon. It is just like fighting the enemy in combat by throwing a bomb that was never detonated; it is completely powerless!

The sword of the spirit is your only offensive weapon in spiritual warfare – all other weapons are defensive i.e. they cover you from the enemy's attack but the sword is literally used to launch attacks against the enemy. Remember, the angels of the Lord respond to voice of His words. When you speak the Word of God that is stored up in your heart and you open your mouth by praying according to these scriptures, victory is yours just like our Lord responded back to Satan's attack in Matthew 4 by answering only with "it is written" bombshells. Our King was also described severally in the final battle as having a sword proceeding out of his mouth.

> **Revelation 18:15** - *Now out of His* **mouth** *goes a sharp* **sword**, *that with it He should strike the nations. And He Himself will rule them with a rod of iron. He Himself treads the winepress of the fierceness and wrath of Almighty God.*

**6. Shoe of the Gospel:** The shoe of the preparation of the gospel of peace is the readiness to defend the faith. The Bible says in Isaiah 52:7,

> *How beautiful upon the mountains are the feet of him who brings good news, Who proclaims peace, Who brings glad tidings of good things, Who proclaims salvation, Who says to Zion, "Your God reigns!"*

Paul said, *"Woe is me if I preach not the gospel"* (1 Corinthians 9:16). The Lord has committed to us the ministry of Reconciliation. He wanted man restored back to glory so much that He sent His only Son whom He loved to die for you and I. 2 Corinthians 5:17-21 says,

> *Therefore, if anyone is in Christ, he is a new creation; old things have passed away; behold, all things have become new. Now all things are of God, who has reconciled us to Himself through Jesus Christ, and has given us the ministry of reconciliation, that is, that God was in Christ reconciling the world to Himself, not imputing their trespasses to them, and has committed to us the word of reconciliation. Now then, we are ambassadors for Christ, as though God were pleading through us: we implore you on Christ's behalf, be reconciled to God. For He made Him who knew no sin to be sin for us, that we might become the righteousness of God in Him.*

In order to win people over to our God we must share the gospel with them or how will they hear except there is a preacher? Someone prayed or preached you in. It is time to share that personal testimony of conversion. Preaching the good news to other people gives you an edge in prayer and spiritual warfare because He said after you do His work and run with the Father's passion for reconciliation, you will ask anything and the Father will grant it to you.

**John 14:12-14** - *You did not choose Me, but I chose you and appointed you that you should go and bear fruit, and that your fruit should remain, that whatever you ask the Father in My name He may give you.*

**7. Prayer and Supplication:** Prayer and supplication is the seventh weapon of our warfare; it is the all time ballistic weapon of mass destruction! The devil hates the believer who loves to pray because prayer brings in the host of heaven and propels divine intervention. Prayer moves God's angels into action especially when praying according to scriptures.

**Psalm 103:20** - *Bless the Lord, you His angels, who excel in strength, who do His word, heeding the voice of His word.*

The efficacy of prayer in spiritual warfare is that it empowers God's angels into action to fight on our behalf. When Peter attacked Marcus (the servant of the high priest) when he came to arrest Jesus in the garden of Gethsemane, Jesus said in Matthew 26:53,

*Or do you think that I cannot now* **pray** *to my father, and he will provide me with more than twelve* **legions of angels**?

So that means you can pray and a militant company of angels will be deployed immediately because as Jesus is, so are we in this world.

You must learn to pray according to His will and His will is the Word – the Bible.

**1 John 5:14-15** - *Now this is the confidence that we have in Him, that if we ask anything according to His will, He hears us. [15] And if we know that He hears us, whatever we ask, we know*

*that we have the petitions that we have asked of Him.*

You must take the Word and put it in your mouth. When you learn how to pray according to the Word of God, you have mastered how to command His angels. You can deploy angels to specific places by praying in the Holy Ghost and praying out scriptures. It is that simple!

The higher level of prayer is praise. Praise is prayer multiplied. It is uncommon faith to praise even when the situation is contrary. Praise compels His divine presence and provokes angelic presence. Every time you look through scriptures, you will find angels fighting battles on behalf of God's people when they key into the advanced level of prayer called praise. It works like dynamite!

**REFLECTION:**
*Father Lord, make me battle ready. Clothe me with the spiritual armory for battle and baptize me with the power that cannot be insulted in Jesus' name.*

# 8
# *Prayer Warfare*

## WHAT IS PRAYER?

IN ORDER TO DELVE DEEPER into the secret of spiritual warfare, we must understand prayer properly. Prayer is not just a spiritual exercise needed to fulfill a religious obligation. Prayer is a two-way communication between God and man. If it is one way, it is not dialogue but a monologue. PRAYER IS NOT about asking God for things all the time; it is not a grocery list of things you want or need. It is about enforcing God's will on the earth. All the patriarchs of old who made a mark in their generation were men or women of prayer. Daniel prayed, Esther prayed, Hannah prayed, Elijah prayed and our Lord Jesus loved to pray.

Prayer is a dynamic sweet communion – empowering and liberating. It is not a chore or some religious obligation to fulfill. When I pray, I am loving my Father! When I pray, I'm addressing specific situations and taking over nations. When I pray, I'm crushing the devil. When I pray, I'm speaking God's words to strengthen my heart. No wonder Jesus prayed all the time! Jesus prayed and had a sweet prayer life so much that the disciples desired to have the same.

**Luke 11:1** - *Now it came to pass, as He was praying in a certain place, when He ceased, that one of His disciples said to Him, "Lord, teach us to pray, as John also taught his disciples."*

## PRAYER OPENS DOORS AND GATES!

The only One who can open the ancient doors is Jesus and He grants us access through the key of prayer. The prayer of the righteous causes ancient captivities to be broken.

**Psalm 24:7-10** - *Lift up your heads, O you gates! And be lifted up, you everlasting doors! And the King of glory shall come in. Who is this King of glory? The Lord strong and mighty, the Lord mighty in battle. Lift up your heads, O you gates! Lift up, you everlasting doors! And the King of glory shall come in. Who is this King of glory? The Lord of hosts, He is the King of glory. Selah.*

This truth is also confirmed in Isaiah 26:2,

*Open the gates, That the righteous nation which keeps the truth may enter in.*

Jesus conquered the power of darkness and disgraced them on the cross of Calvary. He made a nonentity of death and disarmed the power of the grave. He is the only legitimate doorway into the spirit realm. There many other illegal doors and ways like witchcraft, necromancers, sorcery and astrology but the only one that leads to God's realm is Jesus Christ.

**John 14:6**- *Jesus said to him, "I am the way, the truth, and the life. No one comes to the Father except through Me.*

There are many religions that promise access to the spirit world but the end is death and destruction. Jesus has the keys of all the realms and Isaiah 22:22 says,

> *The key of the house of David has been laid on his shoulder; So he shall open, and no one shall shut; And he shall shut, and no one shall open.*

Whatever He shuts can never be opened again. If He shuts a case in heaven's court, no earthly judge or satanic magistrate can open it again. He said that we can enforce this key on the earth through prayers.

> **Matthew 16:19** - *And I will give you the keys of the kingdom of heaven, and whatever you bind on earth will be bound in heaven, and whatever you loose on earth will be loosed in heaven.*

Prayer opens the door of utterance and mysteries of Christ; you must not remain quiet because a prayer-less Christian is a powerless Christian!

> **Colossians 4:2-3** - *Continue in prayer, and watch in the same with thanksgiving; Withal praying also for us, that God would open unto us a door of utterance. (KJV)*

## PRAYER MOVES MOUNTAINS!

Prayer can move mountains of affliction. Although a mountain can be a source of refuge and protection (according to Psalms 125:1-2) or a place of intimate spiritual encounter (as described in Hebrews 12:22-24), in this chapter we are addressing mountains of obstruction.

**Mark 11:22-24** - *Jesus answered and said to them, "Have faith in God or have the God kind of faith - For assuredly, I say to you, whoever says to this mountain, 'Be removed and be cast into the sea,' and does not doubt in his heart, but believes that those things he says will be done, he will have whatever he says. Therefore I say to you, whatever things you ask when you pray, believe that you receive them, and you will have them.*

Just like civil engineers need to cut through a rock or mountain of obstruction by blasting through with controlled explosives, we use the Word of God as our explosive to blast through obstructions. Prayer can break longstanding mountains of delay, limitations, challenges, stagnation, barrenness and struggling. In Job 28:9, wisdom is described as the One who overturns the mountains at the roots. Do you know that you can address the works of creation with your mouth?

**Deuteronomy 32:1** - *Give ear, O heavens, and I will speak; And hear, O earth, the words of my mouth.*

**Genesis 1:1, 3** - *In the beginning God created the heavens and the earth. Then God said, "Let there be light"; and there was light.*

The Bible says in John 1:1-3,

*In the beginning was the Word, and the Word was with God, and the Word was God. He was in the beginning with God. All things were made through Him, and without Him nothing was made that was made.*

Paraphrasing Mark 11:23-24, Jesus said if you desire a good thing and believe in your heart, you will say to the mountain,

"Be removed" and you will have whatever you say. Also, 2 Corinthians 4:13 says that since we have the same spirit of faith, according to what is written, "I believed and therefore I spoke," we also believe and therefore speak. According to Hebrews 10:23, we must hold fast the confession of our hope without wavering, for He who promised is faithful. The proof of your faith is the word you speak from your mouth.

What are the mountains you are experiencing in your personal life? Is it a delay in marital destiny or childbearing? Are you on a long waiting list of immigration process or you are not even on the list for consideration at all? Are you stagnated by unseen forces or do you see a trend of failure at the edge of breakthrough? What is that mountain? You can start by addressing it today! I must tell you this – it may look as if there is no evident effect when you start addressing your mountain but keep at it daily and you will break down the resistance against your destiny. Remember, the mountains didn't just show up yesterday; they are ancient mountains. And like the civil engineers navigating obstructions, you must apply controlled explosives.

The Word of God has creative powers. God saw darkness and God said, "Let there be light" and He began to see good things. Genesis 1 recorded a series of "God said" and "God saw" experiences. If you have been seeing a lot of bondage and captivity around you, then you must speak the things you desire into effect. You must learn to say what you want to see. You must learn to speak to the situation and address it by the word of faith.

**Hebrews 11:3** - *By faith we understand that the worlds were framed by the word of God, so that the things which are seen were* *not made of things which are visible. He framed or created the world by His words.*

Hebrews 1:3 also confirms that He upholds all things created by the word of His power! The Word of God that works like dynamite is the one that is powered by faith. There is a right mix of the Word and faith to produce your desired results.

**Hebrews 4:2** - *For indeed the gospel was preached to us as well as to them; but the word which they heard did not profit them, not being mixed with faith in those who heard it.*

Hebrews 4:12 says that the Word of God is quick and powerful, sharper than any two-edged sword! The word of faith in our mouth is what destroys mountains and the Word of God is also referred to as the gospel of Christ; it carries tremendous power!

**Romans 1:16-17** - *For I am not ashamed of the gospel of Christ* **(the word)** *for it is the power of God to salvation for everyone who believes, for the Jew first and also for the Greek. For in it the righteousness of God is revealed from faith to faith; as it is written, "The just shall live by faith."* (Emphasis mine)

## WATCH YOUR MOUTH!

Your mouth is a power-center; God has ordained that the enemy be cheaply defeated through the device of the mouth.

**Psalm 8:2** - *Out of the mouth of babes and nursing infants You have ordained strength, Because of Your enemies, That You may silence the enemy and the avenger.*

It is also written that this is the victory that overcomes the world even our faith. The word is a double-edged sword (Hebrews 4:12); it is a weapon in the mouth of the believer (Ephesians 6:17). At age 3, the eagle sheds its black beak for a golden one. That is how you differentiate a young eagle from an adult eagle. Your mouth must become seasoned with the word of truth– the sword of the spirit!

> **Luke 21:15** - *For I will give you a mouth and wisdom which all your adversaries will not be able to contradict or resist.*

God speaking in Psalm 81:10 said, "I am the Lord your God, Who brought you out of the land of Egypt; Open your mouth wide, and I will fill it." You must learn to use this weapon well and to your own advantage.

> **Proverbs 18:20-21** - *A man's stomach shall be satisfied from the fruit of his mouth; From the produce of his lips he shall be filled. Death and life are in the power of the tongue, And those who love it will eat its fruit.*

Because your word carries so much power, you must learn not to use your words carelessly .

> **Psalm 141:3** - *Set a guard, O Lord, over my mouth; Keep watch over the door of my lips.*

Don't throw words around carelessly. A believer who speaks carelessly can be likened to a soldier that fires missiles carelessly without having any target. He could end up hurting himself or his loved ones and eventually say, "I didn't mean it." By then, the damage would have already been done; lives lost or injuries incurred.

Here are some scriptures regarding our mouth:

**Proverbs 6:2** - *You are snared by the words of your mouth; You are taken by the words of your mouth.*

**Proverbs 10:11** - *The mouth of the righteous is a well of life, But violence covers the mouth of the wicked.*

**Proverbs 12:14** - *A man will be satisfied with good by the fruit of his mouth, And the recompense of a man's hands will be rendered to him.*

Whether you speak good or bad, you will reap the results.

**Proverbs 13:2-3** - *A man shall eat well by the fruit of his mouth, But the soul of the unfaithful feeds on violence. He who guards his mouth preserves his life, But he who opens wide his lips shall have destruction.*

If you have a problem with verbal impropriety, you need to ask for the fire of the Holy Spirit to touch your mouth today like He touched the mouth of the prophet in Isaiah 6:7,

*And he touched my mouth with it (a live coal of fire) and said: Behold, this has touched your lips; Your iniquity is taken away, And your sin purged. (Emphasis mine)*

I pray for everyone reading this book to begin to speak right and not wrong. We must all learn to speak health and not sickness. We must speak life and not death. Start speaking abundance instead of poverty and use your mouth to promote the works of your hands instead of reinforcing what the economy is saying or what the enemy is doing.

Every time God called a man to a higher place, He dealt with the mouth.

> **Jeremiah 1:9-10** - *Then the Lord put forth His hand and touched my mouth, and the Lord said to me: "Behold, I have put My words in your mouth. ¹⁰See, I have this day set you over the nations and over the kingdoms, To root out and to pull down, To destroy and to throw down, To build and to plant."*

Ezekiel, Moses and Isaiah are all examples of this.

**REFLECTION**:
*Father Lord, give me a mouth and a wisdom that the adversary cannot withstand or refute. Baptize my tongue with Holy Ghost fire!*

# 9
# *Praise Warfare*

PRAISE WARFARE IS ANOTHER crucial weapon in spiritual warfare. Paul and Silas were locked up in prison after they had cast out a demon of divination out of a girl. Their praise brought heaven down because we know that God inhabits the praises of His people. We can see this clearly depicted in the account of victory written in Acts 16:25-26.

> *But at midnight Paul and Silas were praying and singing hymns to God, and the prisoners were listening to them.* [26] *Suddenly there was a great earthquake, so that the foundations of the prison were shaken; and immediately all the doors were opened and everyone's chains were loosed.*

I love the fact that earthquakes usually occur when God shows up on a scene. God is the Captain of the Angelic Armies and He is called Jehovah Sabaoth – the Lord of Host. When He comes down from His abode, He comes down with a shout and the voice of the trumpet. An entourage goes before Him sounding an alarm or blowing their sirens. These Holy Ghost sirens usher in tempests and whirlwinds of fire. The fire consumes sin and every work of darkness but empowers every child of light. Demons fear God and cannot stand His presence, so in order to defeat the enemy, you must intensify His manifest presence through your praise. Remember that when the forsaken King Saul was tormented by evil spirits, he sent for David to get refreshed in 1 Samuel 16:23,

*And so it was, whenever the spirit from God was upon Saul, that David would take a harp and play it with his hand. Then Saul would become refreshed and well, and the distressing spirit would depart from him.*

The secret to his momentary relief was the praise that compels God's divine presence. Divine presence and demonic presence cannot co-exist.

Demons flee before the presence of the Most High and when God shows up, His entourage announce with trumpets of thunder. You will hear sirens of earthquakes and the fiery chariots with strong winds coming down with Him. How can any evil company stand that? They tremble at the presence of the Lord of Host! There was also a time of great distress in Judah when Jehoshaphat and the people went before the Lord in exuberant praise – all their enemies were defeated.

**2 Chronicles 20:20-22** – *So they rose early in the morning and went out into the Wilderness of Tekoa; and as they went out, Jehoshaphat stood and said, "Hear me, O Judah and you inhabitants of Jerusalem: Believe in the LORD your God and you shall be established; believe His prophets, and you shall prosper."* [21] *And when he had consulted with the people, he appointed those who should sing to the LORD, and who should praise the beauty of holiness, as they went out before the army and were saying: "Praise the LORD, For His mercy endures forever."* [22] *Now when they began to sing and to praise, the LORD set ambushes against* *the people of Ammon, Moab, and Mount Seir, who had come against Judah; and they were defeated.*

If you can engage the instrument of praise, you will scatter and defeat any demonic gang-up. Remember the mad man of Gadara – the demons in him were a legion. Jesus also mentioned this when he was teaching about evil spirits that they usually don't like to act alone especially if they have been defeated once.

> **Luke 11:24-26** - *When an unclean spirit goes out of a man, he goes through dry places, seeking rest; and finding none, he says, 'I will return to my house from which I came.' ²⁵ And when he comes, he finds it swept and put in order. ²⁶ Then he goes and takes with him seven other spirits more wicked than himself, and they enter and dwell there; and the last state of that man is worse than the first.*

Jesus actually taught about this phenomenon after he had just dealt with a mute and deaf spirit tormenting a boy in Luke 11:14-23. He was constantly healing the sick and casting out demons during His earthly ministry and gave His disciples the power to do the same so much that they came back rejoicing that evil spirits or demons were subject to them in His name,

> *And He was casting out a demon, and it was mute. So it was, when the demon had gone out, that the mute spoke; and the multitudes marveled. ¹⁵ But some of them said, "He casts out demons by Beelzebub, the ruler of the demons."¹⁶ Others, testing Him, sought from Him a sign from heaven. ¹⁷ But He, knowing their thoughts, said to them: "Every kingdom divided against itself is brought to desolation, and a house divided against a house falls. ¹⁸ If Satan also is divided against himself, how will his*

*kingdom stand? Because you say I cast out demons by Beelzebub.*
*¹⁹ And if I cast out demons by Beelzebub, by whom do your sons*
*cast them out? Therefore they will be your judges. ²⁰ But if I cast*
*out demons with the finger of God, surely the kingdom of God*
*has come upon you. ²¹ When a strong man, fully armed, guards*
*his own palace, his goods are in peace. ²² But when a stronger than*
*he comes upon him and overcomes him, he takes from him all his*
*armor in which he trusted, and divides his spoils. ²³ He who is*
*not with Me is against Me, and he who does not gather with Me*
*scatters.*

Jesus empowered every believer to cast out demons. It is a
Do-IT-Yourself ministry. You can do it yourself; the disciples
actually cast out demons before Christ died and resurrected.

**Luke 10:17-20** — *Then the seventy returned with joy, saying,*
*"Lord, even the demons are subject to us in Your name." ¹⁸ And*
*He said to them, "I saw Satan fall like lightning from heaven.*
*¹⁹ Behold, I give you the authority to trample on serpents and*
*scorpions, and over all the power of the enemy, and nothing shall*
*by any means hurt you. ²⁰ Nevertheless do not rejoice in this, that*
*the spirits are subject to you, but rather rejoice because your names*
*are written in heaven."*

## PRAYER IS A BOMB BUT PRAISE IS A DYNAMITE!

Like I love to say, praise is superior to prayer in any spiritual
warfare. When the children of Israel encountered roadblocks
on their way to the promised land, God instructed them by the
Spirit to administer praise explosives!

**Joshua 6:20** - *So the people shouted when the priests blew the*
*trumpets. And it happened when the people heard the sound of*

*the trumpet, and the people shouted with a great shout, that the wall fell down flat. Then the people went up into the city, every man straight before him, and they took the city.*

In warfare, high praise is a weapon.

**Psalm 149:6** - *Let the high praises of God be in their mouth, and a two-edged sword in their hand.*

Like the wall of Jericho, some doors will prove difficult to open. In such cases, you need to BLOW IT DOWN with the dynamite of praise, like Paul and Silas did:

**Acts 16:25-26** - *But at midnight Paul and Silas were praying and singing hymns to God, and the prisoners were listening to them. Suddenly there was a great earthquake, so that the foundations of the prison were shaken; and immediately all the doors were opened and everyone's chains were loosed.*

## RIGHTEOUSNESS + PRAISE = VICTORY

The combination code that the enemy cannot stand or resist is praise from the mouth of the righteous.

**Psalm 118:19-20** - *Open to me the gates of righteousness; I will go through them, And I will praise the Lord. [20] This is the gate of the Lord, Through which the righteous shall enter.*

To break down some doors of resistance and throw down some ancient gates, you need to possess the right key or combination code. The righteousness or right standing we have is not our own or by works but it was bought by the precious blood of the Lamb. His shed blood brought us complete victory forever. The Lamb of God, the Lion of Judah, has prevailed! He spoiled principalities and powers and made an open show of them, disgracing them in it when He died on the cross of Calvary. That blood, according to Colossians 2:15-16, blots out every handwriting of accusation against you and I – making us RIGHTEOUS and JUSTIFIED – just as if we never sinned.

The praise warfare in the book of Joshua 6 demolished the wall of Jericho. The wall of Jericho represents limitations, failures, stagnation and being locked out of one's inheritance. If you utilize the power of strategic praise in spiritual warfare, you will cheaply defeat the enemy and have complete deliverance like the whole city of Jericho was delivered into the hands of Joshua 6:1-27. See verses 20-21 below:

*So the people shouted when the priests blew the trumpets. And it happened when the people heard the sound of the trumpet, and the people shouted with a great shout, that the wall fell down flat. Then the people went up into the city, every man straight before him, and they took the city. $^{21}$ And they utterly destroyed all that was in the city, man and woman, young and old, ox and sheep and donkey, with the edge of the sword.*

**REFLECTION:**
*Father Lord, clothe me with the garment of praise and anoint me with the oil of gladness. Let your praise become a double-edged sword in my mouth in Jesus' name!*

# 10
# Delivered from Sickness

EVERY BORN AGAIN CHILD of God has been completely delivered from sickness through the finished work of Christ Jesus on the cross of Calvary. The Bible records that healing belongs to us as God's children - it is the children's bread (Matthew 15:21-28). After Christ died and was glorified, salvation was extended to everyone – both Jews and Gentiles. Therefore, every born-again child of God qualifies for healing and the complete provision for divine health has been made for our well-being. In fact, the Lord wants every one of us to be in health according to 3 John 1:2,

> *Beloved, I pray that you may prosper in all things and be in health, just as your soul prospers.*

The question now is, why are believers still sick? The simple answer is that the thief comes to steal, kill and destroy (John10:10).. Sickness may be a result of genetic predisposition, ignorance, fear, condemnation, guilt, spiritual attack or retaliation arrows from the kingdom of darkness. Also, it could simply be as a result of disobedience. It may be lifestyle issues such as lack of rest or the general lack of wisdom. There are many reasons why a believer may be sick and it is impossible to cover all the possible causes in this book. What we will focus on is the provision made available in the scriptures to deal with afflictions.

An unbeliever may enjoy divine healing because of God's mercy and the fact that miracles, signs and wonders advertise God's kingdom. But nowhere in the Bible is there a promise for the unsaved to live continually in good health. Divine health is promised only to God's children.

During the lifetime and ministry of Jesus, many people were healed without salvation and the same still happens today. The only problem is that an unbeliever (i.e. a person who has not committed his/her life to Jesus and made Him Lord and Savior) is continually exposed to the perpetual onslaught of the enemy without any covering at all. They may get healed or delivered today, but without the covering of the blood of Jesus, they may become afflicted by the enemy again.

All through scriptures, healing is promised to all who come to Jesus, whether for a day or for a lifetime. But perpetual health is promised to only those who continually abide under the shadow of the Almighty. So, unbelievers may experience a touch of healing today but they are not guaranteed divine health. Divine health is superior to divine healing – healing is for one instance but health is for life. Divine health is truly the heritage of the saved – those who are saved by the blood of Jesus.

Jesus was wounded for our transgressions and bruised for our iniquities. Are you saved? Have you exchanged mortality for immortality? Jesus took the place of you and I for every category of sickness or disease that exists in the medical books. Whether it is psychological, emotional, physical – any affliction of the spirit, soul or body – Jesus paid the price with His own life.

**Isaiah 53:3-5** - *He was despised and rejected and forsaken by men, a Man of sorrows and pains, and acquainted with grief and sickness; and like One from Whom men hide their faces He was despised, and we did not appreciate His worth or have any esteem for Him. ⁴ Surely He has borne our griefs (sicknesses, weaknesses, and distresses) and carried our sorrows and pains [of punishment], yet we [ignorantly] considered Him stricken, smitten, and afflicted by God [as if with leprosy]. ⁵ But He was wounded for our transgressions, He was bruised for our guilt and iniquities; the chastisement [needful to obtain] peace and well-being for us was upon Him, and with the stripes [that wounded] Him we are healed and made whole. (AMP)*

Most diseases are genetically passed from one generation to another. Have you noticed that when you visit the doctor's office, the first information they ask you is your medical history? Genetic diseases are sometimes maintained by evil personalities who make sure that the affliction is passed down through the bloodline. For example, diabetes runs in families, cancer runs in families, anemia is passed on through the blood; liver diseases and kidney problems also. Likewise, some deadly habits are known to pass on from father to son like alcoholism. For example, when someone in a family tree dies of a heart disease, their offspring is said to be at high risks for such a disease.

Some afflictions may be as a result of satanic arrows thrown suddenly at people who may or may not have such afflictions in their family history. This may happen as a result of demonic retaliations or attacks against a bona-fide child of God. Sometimes it can be as a result of spiritual slumber in a believer. Remember the parable of the wheat and tares; when men slept, the enemy came and sowed tares (Matthew 13:24-30). Demonic affliction can also come into someone's life as a result of bitterness. The Bible says the root of bitterness troubles many and you must not give room to the devil through anger.

Sometimes sicknesses come as a direct result of sin (Deuteronomy 28). When idolatry takes place (even in previous generations), the result is generational afflictions passed down from one generation to another. Despite what the root cause of any affliction is, believers have the sword of the spirit (which is the Word of God) that is quicker and sharper than any surgeon's scapula. This Master Surgeon opened and closed up Adam without leaving a scar. He also discharged Lazarus from the hospital of the dead after he had been dead for four days and stinking!

I don't know how stinking that medical condition is today – Jehovah Rapha is present now to heal you permanently in Jesus' name. I do not care what medical verdict was given to you or your loved one – the Great Physician is still in the business of healing the sick and setting the captives free! You can be delivered from that age-long demonic affliction like that daughter of Abraham that Jesus set free from the 18-year bondage of Satan in Luke13:16.

## HEALED BECAUSE OF A DIVINE EXCHANGE:

Jesus wore the crown of thorns for every mental disorder or any affliction that has to do with the brain. He died young so we can enjoy long life. He took all the pain and grief so we can live pain-free lives. He walked in shame and was stripped naked so we can be clothed with honor and dignity. He was rejected so we would be accepted in the beloved. He bled to death so we can have His blood flowing in our veins to remove any genetic poison or disease. He was poked on the side so that our lungs will never fail. He was punished so we can go unpunished. He bore the weight of our guilt and sin. He paid the ultimate price for our iniquity – our inherited ancestral and generational sins, our tendencies or inclination to sin continually. He was wounded for our transgression – our personal wrongdoings. He carried our sorrows and was acquainted with grief. He was brutally abused and torn to shreds so that no one should ever cut us open again. By His stripes we were healed!

If you are not saved, you cannot enjoy this divine exchange at all. It is a finished work perfected by His death on the cross of Calvary. He swallowed up death and removed the sting of the grave so that you and I can live valiantly on earth and when our time allotted (120 years) is done, we can put off our earth suit and walk gallantly into the presence of our King.

He died and rose again and He is seated on the right side of Majesty far above all principalities (Ephesians 1:20-21). Ephesian 2:5-6 records that even when we were dead in trespasses, He made us alive together with Christ. We have been given power and dominion over ancient serpents and disease-causing scorpions. We can walk all over those genetic lions and ancestral demons because of the place we occupy in Him, far above all principalities our powers. Not only that, we have been mandated to cast out demons and heal the sick with this same power! No more sickness and no more disease! You are completely healed and the precious blood of Jesus has nullified every evil medical history or report in your family history. You can boldly declare: I CANNOT BE SICK AND I CANNOT DIE YOUNG IN JESUS' NAME!

## WHY DO EVIL TRENDS PERSIST?

You may be asking, "Now that I'm born again, why am I still experiencing any of these problems?" Some people come from ancestry that was deep in the occult and idol worship. After you gave your life to Christ the consequences of broken covenants set the household demons on rampage. Since they are no longer worshipped, they are out to devour! They are hungry for blood. They want revenge. For example, in some homes the women must practice witchcraft or else they are donated to witchcraft altars resulting in untimely death. In some other families the men must marry more than one wife and if he is a nominal Christian the evil covenant may turn him to a serial monogamist either through widowhood or divorce. A nominal Christian is one who is a Christian only by name and not in practice. A nominal Christian may attend church or even be baptized in water but his walk with God is empty and his altar lacks fire. The enemy toys with such Christians all the time.

The enemy that we face is very legalistic! He knows all the laws and consequences in the book; he enforces it due to our own ignorance. When you notice an evil trend that continues through generations, it is a stronghold and behind the stronghold is a strongman – not human but spiritual! The Bible speaks in the New Testament about demonic strongholds and the strong man;

> **Luke 11:21-22,24-26** - *When a strong man, fully armed, guards his own palace, his goods are in peace. But when a stronger than he comes upon him and overcomes him, he takes from him all his armor in which he trusted, and divides his spoils.*

Look carefully at the context in which the Master spoke; He was talking about demons. He said,

*When an unclean spirit goes out of a man, he goes through dry places, seeking rest; and finding none, he says, 'I will return to my house from which I came.' And when he comes, he finds it swept and put in order. Then he goes and takes with him seven other spirits more wicked than himself, and they enter and dwell there; and the last state of that man is worse than the first.*

If you must stop that evil trend in your own life, family or neighborhood, then you must be ready to wage war! You must activate the power and authority given to bona-fide sons and your life must carry fire. The enemy doesn't give up his territory easily. Jesus said in Mark 3:27,

*No one can enter a strong man's house and plunder his goods, unless he first binds the strong man. And then he will plunder his house.*

The same was repeated in Matthew 12:29. If you read Matthew 12:22-30, you will see that Jesus had just cast out an evil spirit before he made that statement. Brethren! This is no joke! The reason the doctor cannot diagnose that medical problem is because it is not physical at all! The reason why you cannot get ahead into that desired career is because there are spiritual barriers! The reason why you are always broke and borrowing to meet up is because there is an evil altar manned by household wickedness that must be broken down!

Like Jabez, you must wage war against the evil trend in your father's house and your mother's house! And like Gideon, you must follow the Lord's instruction to demolish the evil altars in your father's house. Ask the Holy Spirit to show you the secret of your ancestry; ask Him to show you any unaddressed covenant. You must take back all that the enemy has stolen from you! The Bible calls him a thief, but Jesus has come to restore ALL (John10:10)!

**Proverbs 6:31** - *Yet when he (a thief) is found, he must restore sevenfold; He may have to give up all the substance of his house. (Emphasis mine)*

QUICKLY MAKE A MENTAL LIST OF WHATEVER HAS BEEN STOLEN FROM YOU NOW! If possible, write them down. You are taking everything back! When praying with the prayer points at the back of this book, you will need to mention those specific areas. Like Jabez, you must break every family trend of sorrow that brings shame!

**1 Chronicles 4:9-10** - *Now Jabez was more honorable than his brothers, and his mother called his name Jabez, saying, "Because I bore him in pain." ¹⁰And Jabez called on the God of Israel saying, "Oh, that You would bless me indeed, and enlarge my territory, that Your hand would be with me, and that You would keep me from evil, that I may not cause pain!" So God granted him what he requested.*

The evil altar that troubled Gideon was from his father's house.

**Judges 6:25-27** - *Now it came to pass the same night that the Lord said to him, "Take your father's young bull, the second bull of seven years old, and tear down the altar of Baal that your father has, and cut down the wooden image that is beside it; ²⁶ and build an altar to the Lord your God on top of this rock in the proper arrangement, and take the second bull and offer a burnt sacrifice with the wood of the image which you shall cut down." ²⁷ So Gideon took ten men from among his servants and did as the Lord had said to him. But because he feared his father's household and the men of the city too much to do it by day, he did it by night.*

I will not be sacrificed on the altars of my father's house. My spouse will not be used to appease household idols in Jesus' name! My children shall not be sacrificed on the evil altars of my mother's house!

## GOD HAS NOT FORGOTTEN YOU!

Contrary to what many people think, God has a book of remembrance. Some of us think God has forgotten us – not completely, but rather some specific areas. We keep wondering, when will my turn come? We may even entertain the notion that God is partial or hard to please. We sometimes get angry, murmur or keep a distance because the enemy is promoting those lies that say we don't matter to God. Like the children of Israel, we may even say it is vain to serve the Lord.

> **Malachi 3:16-18** - *Then those who feared the Lord spoke to one another, And the Lord listened and heard them; So a book of remembrance was written before Him For those who fear the Lord And who meditate on His name. <sup>17</sup>"They shall be Mine," says the Lord of hosts, "On the day that I make them My jewels. And I will spare them As a man spares his own son who serves him." <sup>18</sup>Then you shall again discern Between the righteous and the wicked, Between one who serves God And one who does not serve Him.*

For example, you may even say or think that you refused to compromise by taking the easy route in obtaining immigration papers through false means or arranged marriage, still there's nothing positive to show for it! You may be asking, when will He heal me or give me my own spouse? When will I get that long awaited child? You are probably thinking, "God has definitely forgotten me!" Nothing is further from the truth! The Bible says that we are inscribed on the palm of His hands and our walls are continually before Him. How can He forget you? He said nursing mothers may forget but He will never forget you.

> **Isaiah 49:15-16** - *"Can a woman forget her nursing child, And not have compassion on the son of her womb? Surely they may forget, Yet I will not forget you. [16] See, I have inscribed you on the palms of My hands; Your walls are continually before Me.*

The next questions you may have on your mind are, "How long do I have to wait? When will my turn come? Is this prayer thing even going to work or is it another waste of time?" You reader of this book, your time of favor is now!

> **Psalm 102:13** - *You will arise and have mercy on Zion; for the time to favor her, yes, the set time, has come.*

Since the days of John the Baptist, the kingdom of God suffers violence and the violent take it by force (Matthew 11:12). Call the Man of war in faith to take over and fight all the battles on your behalf. You need His divine intervention to override every power and authority that exists to release your breakthroughs.

You cannot afford doubt or mixed feelings. I sincerely believe that today, as you read this book, long-standing issues will receive divine solutions. I strongly believe that it is payday for some individuals, their families and their generation. Many people whose parents labored in slavery will be directly receiving payback from the taskmasters that exploited their forefathers. You are going up to the high places to release blessings that have been delayed so far. You are not going to do it by your own ability but by the power of the risen Christ who sits far above principalities and powers.

God saw the situation the people of Israel were in, and He was moved to take action (Exodus 2:24-25). God is opening the book of remembrance to visit many forgotten cases. It is your turn to be promoted. It is time to get that job. It is your season of fruitfulness and laughter.

**REFLECTION**:
*Father Lord, I walk in perfect health and total liberty by the blood of Jesus. I refuse to walk in the evil trend of my natural bloodline in Jesus' name.*

# 11
# Delivered from Labor and Toiling

YOU WERE CREATED FOR WORK and not labor and Christ has redeemed us from the curse of the law. From the beginning, God intended for us to work and be blessed, not to labor and be stressed. Adam's assignment was very simple. God instructed him to work and tend the garden (Genesis 2:15) but Adam sinned and it brought dire consequences – the ground became cursed. He began to eat from the sweat of his brow.

> **Genesis 2:15** - *Then the Lord God took the man and put him in the Garden of Eden to tend and keep it. [16] And the Lord God commanded the man, saying, "Of every tree of the garden you may freely eat; but of the tree of the knowledge of good and evil you shall not eat, for in the day that you eat of it you shall surely die."*

Adam ate of the forbidden fruit. As long as he followed the Lord's instruction, He succeeded and we can see the extent of his success in Genesis 2:20,

> *So Adam gave names to all cattle, to the birds of the air, and to every beast of the field. But for Adam there was not found a*

*helper comparable to him.*

He walked, talked and thought like the Creator. Until one day he fell and the curse of sweat was activated through disobedience.

> **Genesis 3:17-19** - *Then to Adam He said, "Because you have heeded the voice of your wife, and have eaten from the tree of which I commanded you, saying, 'You shall not eat of it': "Cursed is the ground for your sake; In toil you shall eat of it All the days of your life. Both thorns and thistles it shall bring forth for you, And you shall eat the herb of the field. In the sweat of your face you shall eat bread Till you return to the ground, For out of it you were taken; For dust you are, And to dust you shall return.*

All through scriptures, the descendants of Adam suffered untold hardship and toiling as a result of Adam's fall. Individuals as well as nations have become bound by the curse of toiling and sweating.

Let us take a quick look at an example of the forces of darkness enforcing the curse of hard labor on God's people (the Israelites) in Egypt.

> **Exodus 1:11-14** - *So the Egyptians made the Israelites their slaves. They appointed brutal slave drivers over them, hoping to wear them down with crushing labor. They forced them to build the cities of Pithom and Rameses as supply centers for the king. But the more the Egyptians oppressed them, the more the Israelites multiplied and spread, and the more alarmed the Egyptians became. So the Egyptians worked the people of Israel without mercy. They made their lives bitter, forcing them to mix mortar and make bricks and do all the work in the fields. They were ruthless in all their demands. (NLT)*

Today, believers who by virtue of the Abrahamic covenant should be enjoying the work of their hands are struggling under heavy burdens, just like the children of the covenant. Despite salvation and following God's instructions about finances, many believers are still struggling under the power of the taskmaster. Regardless of their geographical location, many still bear the burden of heavy debt resulting from school loans, credit cards and unfair mortgages. Many are struggling to meet up with responsibilities and feel lost from chasing the Golden Fleece. I have good news for you - God has a golden fleece and it even has a silver lining. He gave this fleece to Gideon to empower him and set him free from the yoke of the Midianites (Judges 6).

The Israelites were abused and vandalized by the terror called the Midianites. Whenever the Israelites planted their crops, marauders from Midian, Amalek, and the people of the east would attack Israel, camping in the land and destroying crops as far away as Gaza. They left the Israelites with nothing to eat, taking all the sheep, goats, cattle, and donkeys. These enemy hordes, coming with their livestock and tents, were as thick as locusts; they arrived on droves of camels too numerous to count. And they stayed until the land was stripped bare. So Israel was reduced to starvation by the Midianites. Then the Israelites cried out to the Lord for help.

The destroyer was given permission to toy with our work and turn it into labor when man fell in the garden (Genesis 3). In the case we just read above (Judges 6), the agents the devil used were the Midianites and Amalekites? They represent the devourer, wasting and destruction; laboring in vain and starvation. They represent emptiness (working so hard and having little or nothing to show for it), the fear of tomorrow and extreme poverty. The Midianites usually wait for the planting to be completed and strikes when it is about time for God's people to harvest the increase.

As Christians, we should not operate under the curse of sweating and toiling because another Adam came – our Lord Jesus Christ. He died for our sins on the cross of Calvary. He redeemed us from the curse of the law and from the curse of sweating and toiling. He started by shedding His blood in another garden called "Gethsemane". He prayed until the capillaries in his head busted and mixed with His sweat and dropped on the ground that was cursed for our sake (Luke 22:44) . He wore the crown of thorns to deliver our lives from sweating and toiling. He proclaimed with a loud voice on the cross, "IT IS FINISHED!" The affliction of sweat is finished! The struggles and toiling is finished! The "working so hard and having little to show for it" is finished! The syndrome of working like an elephant and eating like an ant is finished! The shame of emptiness and poverty is finished! The era of sweating has become the era of sweat-less victories! Enough is enough – no more toiling and struggling.

From now on, you should boldly declare Psalm 90:17,

*And let the beauty of the Lord our God be upon us, And establish the work of our hands for us; Yes, establish the work of our hands.*

Jesus speaking in Matthew 11:28-29 said,

*Come to Me, all you who labor and are heavy laden, and I will give you rest. Take My yoke upon you and learn from Me, for I am gentle and lowly in heart, and you will find rest for your souls.*

Jesus wants you to have rest even while working; rest is a state of mind. You must victoriously personalize and proclaim Isaiah 65:21-23,

> *They shall build houses and inhabit them; They shall plant vineyards and eat their fruit. They shall not build and another inhabit; They shall not plant and another eat; For as the days of a tree, so shall be the days of My people, And My elect shall long enjoy the work of their hands. They shall not labor in vain, Nor bring forth children for trouble; For they shall be the descendants of the blessed of the Lord, And their offspring with them.*

Our enemy doesn't play fair or follow the rules. He is a thief who will stop at nothing to steal from legitimate sons. The Bible says since the days of John the Baptist the kingdom of God suffers violence and the violent take it by force! You must forcefully take back everything he has stolen from you. The enemy knows the entire content of the Bible; he was even quoting scriptures to the Savior Himself in Matthew 4. The Old Testament is filled with laws and repercussions of any misdeed. You know what? The enemy is still busy going around with his cohort maintaining evil altars and carrying out the effects of the curse of the law as stated in Deuteronomy 28. The Bible calls the devil the accuser of the brethren (Revelation 12:10). He enforces the law where God has shown mercy and imposes guilt and condemnation where Christ had made us free.

After Christ died on the cross for you and I, God has been completely appeased and is not mad with mankind anymore. Jesus became the propitiation for our sins for all those who lived before Him and all those who will ever live, till the end of time. Romans 8:1-2 says we no longer operate under the old laws in the book but under a new covenant of the spirit of life! Many of the children of Israel made it out of slavery but never made it to the Promised Land. So also many people today make it out of generational curses but never truly experience the impact of generational blessings! Jesus died so that you and I can enjoy life in abundance! He became a curse so that we can partake of the blessings set apart for the righteous. When you are saved by His blood, you are not half-saved or second or third grade righteous but completely righteous!

> **Galatians 3:13-14** - *Christ has redeemed us from the curse of the law, having become a curse for us for it is written, "Cursed is everyone who hangs on a tree", that the blessing of Abraham might come upon the Gentiles in Christ Jesus, that we might receive the promise of the Spirit through faith.*

In fact, the Bible calls you and I the righteousness of God in Christ Jesus!

> **2 Corinthians 5:21** - *For He made Him who knew no sin to be sin for us, that we might become the righteousness of God in Him.*

Because of Christ Jesus, we have pleased God. See what the Psalmist says about a man who pleases the Lord,

> **Psalm 24:5-6** - *He shall receive blessing from the Lord and righteousness from the God of his salvation. This is the generation [description] of those who seek Him [who inquire of and for Him and of necessity require Him], who seek Your face, O God of Jacob. Selah. (AMP)*

Pause and think about that! The Bible makes it clear that there is a new covenant now promised in Jeremiah 31:29-30, 33:

> *In those days they shall say no more, The fathers have eaten sour grapes, and the children's teeth are set on edge. But everyone shall*

*die for his own iniquity only; every man who eats sour grapes—his own teeth shall be set on edge. But this is the covenant which I will make with the house of Israel: After those days, says the Lord, I will put My law within them, and on their hearts will I write it; and I will be their God, and they will be My people.*

Therefore, I refuse to pay for the sins of my father's house in Jesus' name! My children's teeth will no longer be set on edge for the wickedness of my ancestors in the mighty name of Jesus. I excel where my predecessors failed in Jesus' name! I AM BLESSED BEYOND THE CURSE! I AM LIVING UNDER A NEW COVENANT!

When you make Jesus Christ your Lord and personal savior, you benefit from the fact that Jesus defeated the enemy. He has blotted out all the handwriting of ordinances that the enemy is still carrying around to afflict many. Over 2000 years ago, Jesus died so that we can be blessed and redeemed from the curse of the law. So you are delivered completely from the curse of sweating and toiling!

**REFLECTION**:
***Father Lord, I choose to engage in profitable work from today and I receive the grace to enjoy the work you have assigned to me in life and ministry in Jesus' name.***

# 12
# Delivered from Self

## SELF: THE OLD MAN AND HIS SINFUL NATURE

IN ORDER TO WALK in complete deliverance, "SELF" must be sacrificed on the altar of absolute submission to the Lord. Paul writing to the church in Rome said,

> **Romans 12:1-2** - *I beseech you therefore, brethren, by the mercies of God, that you present your bodies a living sacrifice, holy, acceptable to God, which is your reasonable service. ² And do not be conformed to this world, but be transformed by the renewing of your mind, that you may prove what is that good and acceptable and perfect will of God.*

It is of utmost importance to mortify or kill the flesh, otherwise the enemy will use the flesh to steal from, kill or destroy the believer. The weakness that is not dealt with usually becomes the undoing of the man. Moses lost his opportunity to see the Promised Land because of his anger. Samson lost his greatness and vision due to sexual immorality. David stumbled because of adultery. Uzziah became leprous because of pride. Gehazi lost the opportunity to become the successor of the prophet Elisha with double portion of his anointing due to covetousness and greed; instead, he inherited leprosy for himself and his children after him.

> **Romans 8:18-20** - *For I know that in me (that is, in my flesh) nothing good dwells; for to will is present with me, but how to perform what is good I do not find. ¹⁹ For the good that I will to do, I do not do; but the evil I will not to do, that I practice. ²⁰ Now if I do what I will not to do, it is no longer I who do it, but sin that dwells in me.*

Look closely at the word **SELF**; if spelt backwards it spells **FLES** and when you add the letter "H", it becomes **FLESH**. It is nothing other than the human nature or the old man or the sin nature. It is time for us to move from the sin nature to divine nature.

An example written for us in the Old Testament is about King Uzziah, a king who sought God very early in his life. He became king at the young age of 16. He sought God and did great exploits. The Bible records that as long as he sought the Lord, God made him to prosper.

> **2 Chronicles 26:3-5** - *Uzziah was sixteen years old when he became king, and he reigned fifty-two years in Jerusalem. His mother's name was Jecholiah of Jerusalem. And he did what was right in the sight of the Lord, according to all that his father Amaziah had done. He sought God in the days of Zechariah, who had understanding in the visions of God; and as long as he sought the Lord, God made him prosper.*

He started well by depending on God but he stumbled when he began to depend on self. He became inflated, his ego became supersized and he started to operate in self-confidence, pride and anger which led to self-destruction.

**2 Chronicles 26:16,19** - *But when he was strong his heart was lifted up, to his destruction, for he transgressed against the Lord his God by entering the temple of the Lord to burn incense on the altar of incense. Then Uzziah became furious; and he had a censer in his hand to burn incense. And while he was angry with the priests, leprosy broke out on his forehead, before the priests in the house of the Lord, beside the incense altar.*

What a shame! What calamity for greatness to quickly become such disgrace. This was written for us to learn from. The path of the just is planned to become successively better and brighter. However, in order to finish the race victoriously and defeat our common foe, we must completely destroy "king self" and let King Jesus reign in his place.

The prophet Isaiah could not see God's glory or be sent out for God's purpose until everything Uzziah represented had died.

**Isaiah 6:1-7** - *In the year that King Uzziah died, I saw the Lord sitting on a throne, high and lifted up, and the train of His robe filled the temple. Above it stood seraphim; each one had six wings: with two he covered his face, with two he covered his feet, and with two he flew. And one cried to another and said: "Holy, holy, holy is the Lord of hosts; The whole earth is full of His glory!" And the posts of the door were shaken by the voice of him who cried out, and the house was filled with smoke. So I said: "Woe is me, for I am undone! Because I am a man of unclean lips, And I dwell in the midst of a people of unclean lips; For my eyes have seen the King, The Lord of hosts." Then one of the seraphim flew to me, having in his hand a live coal which he had taken with the tongs from the altar. And he touched my mouth with it, and said: "Behold, this has touched your lips; Your iniquity is taken away, And your sin purged."*

After the purging by fire, self-consciousness translated into God-consciousness. Isaiah could see and hear God's call clearly before the consecration but in Isaiah 6:8 he said,

> *Also I heard the voice of the Lord, saying:"Whom shall I send,And who will go for Us?"Then I said, "Here am I! Send me.*

We must all come to that altar of total consecration and nothing called SELF must remain alive. Paul said to mortify the flesh and he wrote concerning himself that I die daily — not his life but his flesh and all its inordinate affections.

What does Uzziah represent in our lives today? Uzziah is KING SELF and you must get deliverance from KING SELF today!! All the self-worship must die! — self-pride, self-defeat, selfishness, self-loathing or hatred, self-love, self-centeredness, self-approval, self-pity, self-assurance, self-confidence, self-condemnation, self-destruction, self-depreciation, self-indulgence and self-fulfilling prophecy.

Very few self- words have positive meanings e.g. self-discipline and self-esteem; most self- words are either too pitiful or too arrogant. From today, self-consciousness must give way to God-consciousness! Selfishness must become selflessness, we must begin to look away from self and start to look at Jesus, the author and finisher of our faith! Until Uzziah (pride) died Isaiah could not see God's glory. Until self died, God could not send him on his life's mission. Until SELF dies you are not ready to actualize destiny!

The Apostle Paul explained the challenge of self as the inner turmoil or struggle with the sin nature.

**Romans 7:5** - *For when we were in the flesh, the sinful passions which were aroused by the law were at work in our members to bear fruit to death. For I know that in me that is, in my flesh nothing good dwells.*

But praise be to God that it does not end there! Thank God that Paul continued the discussion in the next chapter,

**Romans 8:1-11** - *There is therefore now no condemnation to those who are in Christ Jesus, who do not walk according to the flesh, but according to the Spirit. For the law of the Spirit of life in Christ Jesus has made me free from the law of sin and death. For what the law could not do in that it was weak through the flesh, God did by sending His own Son in the likeness of sinful flesh, on account of sin: He condemned sin in the flesh, that the righteous requirement of the law might be fulfilled in us who do not walk according to the flesh but according to the Spirit. For when we were in the flesh, the sinful passions which were aroused by the law were at work in our members to bear fruit to death. For those who live according to the flesh set their minds on the things of the flesh, but those who live according to the Spirit, the things of the Spirit. For to be carnally minded is death, but to be spiritually minded is life and peace. Because the carnal mind is enmity against God; for it is not subject to the law of God, nor indeed can be. So then, those who are in the flesh cannot please God. But you are not in the flesh but in the Spirit, if indeed the Spirit of God dwells in you. Now if anyone does not have the Spirit of Christ, he is not His. And if Christ is in you, the body is dead because of sin, but the Spirit is life because of righteousness. But if the Spirit of Him who raised Jesus from the dead dwells in you, He who raised Christ from the dead will also give life to your mortal bodies through His Spirit who dwells in you.*

Simply use the power in the Word to separate the flesh from the spirit; the Word is the quickest and sharpest sword (Hebrews 4:12). Know that you are not doing this alone but with the great High priest of our profession.

> **Hebrews 4:14-16** - *Seeing then that we have a great High Priest who has passed through the heavens, Jesus the Son of God, let us hold fast our confession. For we do not have a High Priest who cannot sympathize with our weaknesses, but was in all points tempted as we are, yet without sin. Let us therefore come boldly to the throne of grace, that we may obtain mercy and find grace to help in time of need.*

Enforce the finished work of Christ on the cross over every propensity to stumble and the very innate tendency to sin and carry the guilt or condemnation. Lay aside the weight of sin and run the race of destiny set before you! You will be transformed like Gideon who went from being the poorest and smallest with low self-esteem to becoming who God called him to be – a mighty man of valor, a man of fearless courage. You will be just like Moses who went from being a self-appointed deliverer running away from the law – to being the God-appointed deliverer of God's people. You will be like Jacob who went from being a cheater and supplanter running from his self-deceit to become intimately bold in God's presence and empowered to face himself and ultimately his enemies. You will be empowered and baptized with the fire of the Holy Ghost like Peter; who went from being a coward that denied Christ three times before men to become a bold defender of the truth before thousands of people, leading many more thousands to Christ.

Regardless of your situation, educational or family background, race, gender, history, age, challenges or marital status, God wants to do mighty and wondrous things through you! Today,

He is speaking expressly to you to leave that limitation – SELF. Leave the old man behind and become transformed into the new man that walks in boldness, does exploits for His Kingdom, defeats the powers of darkness and take over territories for the Lord with His holy angels working with you behind the scene.

## GOD IS A MAN OF WAR!

In this battle, you need to understand that the God we serve is a man of war.

> **Exodus 15:3** - *The Lord is a man of war; The Lord is His name.*

> **Isaiah 42:13** - *The Lord shall go forth like a mighty man; He shall stir up His zeal like a man of war. He shall cry out, yes, shout aloud; He shall prevail against His enemies.*

Are you facing unusual battles in your life right now? Does it seem as if you are running from pillar to post or riding on a roller coaster of unending spiritual warfare? Or is it as if all hell broke loose against you? At your waking moments you are fighting forces and at night you experience such intense warfare that it has become too scary to go to sleep. Is your dream life a continuous battle front? Have you been waking up feeling like you were wrestling all night? Jacob wrestled all night and prevailed (Genesis 32:26, 28, 30). You may be saying right now, "But Jacob wrestled with God. The enemy is contending with me all the time and it feels like a never-ending battle." Don't worry! The Lion of Judah has prevailed.

> **Revelation 5:5** - *But one of the elders said to me, "Do not weep. Behold, the Lion of the tribe of Judah, the Root of David, has prevailed.*

As a son of the Most High, you need not fight any battles on your own anymore. The battle belongs to your God.

> **2 Chronicles 20:15** - *And he said, "Listen, all you of Judah and you inhabitants of Jerusalem, and you, King Jehoshaphat! Thus says the Lord to you: 'Do not be afraid nor dismayed because of this great multitude, for the battle is not yours, but God's.*

I AM SAYING THE SAME TO YOU NOW AS IN THE DAYS OF JEHOSHAPHAT - ***Thus says the Lord to you: 'Do not be afraid nor dismayed because of this great battle: for the battle is not yours, but God's.***

If you submit to His leading and instructions through the Holy Spirit, you will gain sweat-less victory over every attack of the enemy. You will win all the battle arrayed against you by the satanic host.

He is the Man of war; He is equipped for battle and conquers each time. I love this Man of war so much because all I need to do is cry out to Him and He will show up with His fearful troop! Your assignment has been made very simple! You are simply expected to exercise the authority in spiritual warfare through the instrumentality of prayer. Ephesians 6:18 mentions the all-time ballistic weapon of mass destruction as prayer,

> *Praying always with all prayer and supplication in the Spirit, being watchful to this end with all perseverance and supplication for all the saints.*

Jesus said he has given us power and authority to trample upon all the powers of the enemy (Luke 10:19). However, this power and authority is only available to those who have accepted Jesus as their Lord and Savior. If you are saved already, you are more than ready for prayer warfare; praise the Lord! But if you are not saved, please do not let this moment to engage this Mar of war in your daily battles pass you. All through this book and throughout Scriptures, we can conclude that the guarantee for victory against the enemy is only for the saved – those who have made Jesus Christ their Lord and Savior. If you are not yet saved, I want to give you another opportunity to engage this Veteran of War and the Captain of salvation in your battles. Please say this simple prayer out loud:

***Lord Jesus, I accept You as my Lord and Savior. Deliver me and save me from my sins. Forgive me and wash me with Your blood. Set me free from every lawful captivity and generational battle. Take over my battles from today. Now I know that I am born again to serve the living God in Jesus' name. Amen!***

Welcome to the family of God! Now that you are born again and translated from the kingdom of darkness to the kingdom of His marvelous light, you are ready to launch attacks against the enemy using the sword of the Spirit. The sword is powered by faith and the righteousness you have acquired through the precious blood of the Lamb. You can now freely engage the Mighty Man of war anytime for your deliverance and the deliverance of others around you!

If you said this prayer, I would like to hear from you. Please contact me through the details at the back of this book. I also encourage you to use the prayer guides and scripture references in the Appendix of this book.

# *Conclusion*

## PRAYER DELIVERS US FROM AFFLICTION

PRAYER DELIVERED HANNAH from years of barrenness and ridicule.

> **1 Samuel 1:11,20** - *Then she made a vow and said, "O Lord of hosts, if You will indeed look on the affliction of Your maidservant and remember me, and not forget Your maidservant, but will give Your maidservant a male child, then I will give him to the Lord all the days of his life, and no razor shall come upon his head." ²⁰So it came to pass in the process of time that Hannah conceived and bore a son, and called his name Samuel, saying, "Because I have asked for him from the Lord."*

**You can be delivered as well!**

Prayer delivered Jabez from a life of dishonor and stagnation.

> **1 Chronicles 4:9-10** - *Now Jabez was more honorable than his brothers, and his mother called his name Jabez, saying, "Because I bore him in pain." And Jabez called on the God of Israel saying, "Oh, that You would bless me indeed, and enlarge my territory, that Your hand would be with me, and that You would keep me from evil, that I may not cause pain!" So God granted him what he requested.*

**You can receive your own turnaround as well!**

Prayer unveiled the supernatural nature of Christ again and again! On the mountain of transfiguration as Jesus prayed, the appearance of His face was altered, and His robe became white and glistening.

> **Luke 9:29** - *As He prayed, the appearance of His face was altered, and His robe became white and glistening.*

Prayer empowers you for exploits because the Bible shows us what happened to Jesus when He came down from that time of prayer.

> **Luke 9:37** - *Now it happened on the next day, when they had come down from the mountain, that a great multitude met Him.*

Whenever you spend time in prayer, you are tapping into the divine nature of Elohim. The demons cannot stand your face. Remember when Moses came down from the mountain as well, his face shone too. So much so that the people could not look him in the face. You need to pray your way into that realm of supernatural empowerment. You cannot achieve this by praying "touch-and-go" prayers but by spending quality time in God's presence. The more you spend time in His presence, the more you will look like Him. The more you rub minds with Him, the more you will think like Him. The more you spend time studying His words, the more you will talk like Him.

If you take a closer look at the account of the transfiguration, you will see that there was something peculiar about the number of days mentioned in the scriptures. I strongly believe that Jesus had been fasting and praying for about a week (7 days) because the three different accounts mentioned "after six days" or "about eight days". My question is, six days after what? And I love the fact that Luke 9 told us exactly what He was doing. The transfiguration was not just a random incidence at all – Jesus was praying! I want to carefully add that He may have been fasting as well because the Bible to keep mentioning the number of days in all three scriptures:

**Matthew 17:1-2** - *Now after six days Jesus took Peter, James, and John his brother, led them up on a high mountain by themselves; and He was transfigured before them. His face shone like the sun, and His clothes became as white as the light.*

**Mark 9:2-3** - *Now after six days Jesus took Peter, James, and John, and led them up on a high mountain apart by themselves; and He was transfigured before them. His clothes became shining, exceedingly white, like snow, such as no launderer on earth can whiten them.*

**Luke 9:28-29** - *Now it came to pass, about eight days after these sayings, that He took Peter, John, and James and went up on the mountain to pray. As He prayed, the appearance of His face was altered, and His robe became white and glistening.*

As you engage the strategy outlined in God's Word accompanied with fasting and prayer, I believe that you will emerge with glistening robe that will blind the enemy forever. Spiritual warfare requires empowerment and we can see that empowerment comes from the Lord. The Psalmist said power belongs to Him! It takes a level of light to defeat darkness and I dare say that Jesus the Light we need to destroy every form of darkness.

If Jesus prayed and fasted while He walked this earthly realm, I think we need to follow His perfect example. He came to show us how to live the supernatural life. The grace He gave us is not meant to lay dormant in us; instead we need to activate and unleash that power to our world. How? Through prayer and fasting! The Chosen Fast described in Isaiah 58:6-12 says your light will dawn in darkness; this is God's prescription for deliverance.

You can be delivered just as He delivered me from the jaws of the lion.

*Appendix:*
*Sample Prayer Points*

## PRAYER OF DELIVERANCE

Read the following scriptures out loud:
* Psalm 2:1-end, Psalm 3:1-end, Psalm 4:1-end, Psalm 70:1-end
* Isaiah 49:24-26, Isaiah 54:14-15&17, Deuteronomy 32:39-42
* Luke 10:19, Ephesians 1:20-21, Ephesians 2:4-6, Ephesians 6:10-18
* Colossians 2:14-15 and Colossians 3:3

Study and meditate on these for personal development:
* Roman 8:1-end and Galatians 4:1-7

Confess any known or unknown sin (generational or ancestral).

Engage the Weapon of praise and worship - Psalm 100:4

### Prayer Points

1. Thank you Jesus for saving me by Your precious blood of everlasting covenant.

2. Thank You for forgiving my sins and washing me clean by the blood of Jesus.

3. Thank You for blotting out every generational and ancestral sin by the blood.

4. I break every oath and evil covenant with family idols in Jesus' name.

5. I cancel every evil dedication to idols and spirit of dead people by the blood of Jesus.

6. I plead the blood of Jesus and receive complete forgiveness for all sins from my youth.

7. I command all the property of the strongman in my life or my dream to catch fire and be consumed in Jesus' name.

8. I denounce every covenant binding me to any evil altar to be neutralized by the blood of Jesus.

9. I command every evil rope drawing me back to square one to break and perish in Jesus' name.

10. Every evil covenant made at my birth must be broken in Jesus' name.

11. Every household wickedness or witchcraft pursuing me drown in the red sea of the blood of Jesus.

12. Father, anoint me with fire and set me apart for Your glory.

13. Father, heal me and I shall be healed! Save me and I shall be saved.

14. Lord, deliver me from the enemy that is too strong for me.

15. Father, show my adversaries that You are the mighty man of war!

16. Lord, let Your militants angels surround me at all times.

17. I cover myself with the blood of Jesus.

18. I hide myself under the shadow of the Almighty.

19. I shall not die but live to declare the glory of God in the land of the living.

20. My destiny receive power to shine as a star of the Most High God.

21. Thank You Lord for resurrection power working through my body for supernatural strength.

Give thanks for answered prayers.


## DELIVERANCE FROM SATANIC YOKES
(Breaking Evil Trends)

1. Thank You Lord for the blood of sprinkling that speaks better things than the blood of Abel. Thank You for being my defender and my helper.

2. Thank You for saving me to the uttermost by the blood of everlasting covenant and for using the salvation in Christ Jesus to rewrite my family history.

3. Thank You for the blood of Jesus that speaks total emancipation for my family and complete freedom from all evil trends, evil altars and evil dedications!

4. I receive total and complete freedom from every evil ancestral and generational covenant. I break every curse of the law working against me by the blood of Jesus.

5. I free myself, my husband and my children from every stronghold of dark covenants by the blood of Jesus. I blot out the handwriting of ordinances contrary to me and my family by the blood of Jesus.

6. I bind every strongman of my father's house, my mother's house and my in-laws house in Jesus' name. I release my goods from the stronghold of the enemy and I render all evil habitation desolate in Jesus' name!

7. I dismantle every evil altar erected on my behalf from generations past affecting my journey in life and I receive the spirit of grace and supplication to engage in spiritual warfare in Christ Jesus.

8. Baptize me with Holy Ghost fire that swallows up evil trends and consume evil chains. Father, envelope with Your power that cannot be insulted in the mighty name of Jesus.

9. I break every power of witchcraft operating openly or covertly against me. Holy Ghost; Captain of the Host! Rain fire, rain thunder, rain hailstorm in the camp of my adversary today!

10. Anoint me for uncommon breakthrough in my career, ministry and marriage. I break free from every evil chain or cords of dark and evil covenant affecting my health, finances, marriage or destiny in Jesus' name.

11. Holy Ghost expose every dark secrets of my fathers house, mothers house and my in-laws house and disgrace them! Turn me to Your firebrand battle-axe and use me to break down satanic strongholds!

12. Father, anoint me as an arrow in Your mighty hands to help others that are oppressed by the enemy! Use me to deliver many from the prison of the enemy.

Give thanks to God for answered prayers.

# DELIVERANCE FROM SATANIC OBSTRUCTIONS
(Crushing Evil Mountains)

1. Thank You Lord for the awesome privilege to be alive and well on this first day of the month. Thank You for giving me the opportunity to stand in Your presence.

2. Thank You for the precious blood of Jesus that speaks salvation for me and my entire household. Thank You for giving me a mouth and wisdom that breaks down the resistance of the enemy.

3. Thank You for the spirit of revelation on my prayer altar and for the power in the word that works through faith demolishing mountains by their roots.

4. Anoint my tongue with the Holy Ghost fire and let my mouth be sanctified for Your glory. I speak with the tongue of the learned and I decree with the same power as Elohim; as I say it so shall it be in Jesus' name.

5. I command you mountain of affliction (name it and be specific) to be removed and cast into the sea! I am unstoppable and unmolestable in Jesus' name.  I trample down every mountain of resistance slowing me down my journey in life.

6. You mountain of financial difficulties, I defy you now in the name of Jesus! He became poor so that I can be rich; He became cursed so that I can be blessed in the order of Abraham. You spirit of chronic and generational poverty get out of my life in Jesus' name.

7. Mountain of affliction be removed in Jesus' name - the blood of Jesus is against you. The sicknesses that run in the blood-line I curse you now to be withered to your root in Jesus' name. Noisome pestilence must flee, common and uncommon diseases I rebuke your operation in my household!

8. Mountain of resistance to my church and ministry be removed in Jesus' name; every spirit of unbelief and all the mystery of iniquity working in this land be destroyed by the power in the blood of Jesus! Deaf ears be opened, blind eyes begin to see and all hardened hearts receive the touch of salvation and see Jesus!

9. Ancient mountains lift up your heads! I say you great mountains be overturned by the roots in the name of Jesus - My destiny must shine! My life must attract color and my journey will not be diverted or wasted; I bring forth my fruits in season according to Psalm 1:3.

10. Every unrepentant adversary and stubborn enemy standing in my path be grounded to powder in Jesus' name! You stubborn affliction called barrenness, miscarriage, misfortune, lack, shame, pain, debt, joblessness, destiny time wasters catch fire!

11. My destiny helpers arise! My divine promoters locate me for divine encounters. All my teachers and recommenders must locate me this month in the name of Jesus. Nothing will stop me - no sickness, no failure, no sorrow, no depression, no weapon fashioned against me shall prosper!

12. Divine opportunities begin to pursue me as I make quick progress in life! I cannot be stopped by household wickedness or territorial darkness. The Captain of the Host is lighting my path and crushing every resistance on my way to greatness!

Give thanks for answered prayers!

# DELIVERANCE FROM SATANIC ROAD BLOCKS
(Ancient Gates Be Lifted!)

1. Thank You Lord for open heavens over my life and my entire household today. Thank You for showing me the secret of spiritual warfare.

2. Thank You for saving me by the blood of Jesus and washing me clean from all my sins. Thank You for the name of Jesus; that opens stubborn doors and dismantle strange doors.

3. Thank You for giving to me the keys of the kingdom so that whatever I bind on earth is bound and whatever I lose on earth is loosed!

4. Thank You for the keys of David that shut the gates of hell forever and open the gates of heaven to me and my family!

5. I thank You for giving me the free access of righteousness through the blood of Jesus; from today I gain expedited access to answered prayers through the keys of revelation and praise.

6. Heavenly Father, grant me access to heaven's never-ending provision and supplies for all my daily needs. Move me from the realms of barely enough to the level of blessing to others!

7. Father Lord, open Your heavenly food pantry and feed me with angels' food. Satisfy me with the bread of Your word, the meat of revelation and the rivers of Your wisdom.

8. Father Lord, loosen the armory of kings before me and let me become a custodian of kingdom treasuries held up in the hand of kings. As this year runs to an end, open the treasuries of kings to me. Let the hidden riches of secret places be released to me and my family.

9. Captain of the Host! Let Your angels defend me from strange battles and take back from the adversary every stolen blessing for me. Bombard strange doors and disarm wicked

doorkeepers holding down my blessings!

10. My prayer altar catch fire, Holy Ghost fire fill my soul. My spirit receive a fresh baptism of fire for empowered prayer life! I enjoy sweet communion and intercession for others in Jesus' name.

11. Every door that has been shut before me in my career, ministry, business or academic let them begin to open automatically before me in the mighty name of Jesus. I dismantle evil doors and shatter satanic gates in Jesus' name!

12. Through the keys of David I gain access to palaces of kings and secret treasures of nations that my family had never experienced before me. Use me to rewrite my family history.

13. My prayer life must align with heavens agenda from today as angels obey the decrees issued through my prayers in Jesus' name. Send out Your militant angels to defeat every adversary of my greatness and success in life.

14. Let me experience angelic ministration as a daily occurrence in my life. Open my eyes through insight to see their activities all around me as an heir of salvation.

15. Increase is mine, blessings are mine in Jesus' name. Favor of kings and experts in my field becomes my portion, doors of opportunity that leads to greatness open to me by fire and by force.

16. I operate with understanding in my prayer life from today to release angels on assignment for the expansion of the kingdom of our Lord Jesus Christ.

17. I tap into the grace of our Lord Jesus and the anointing to excel in all my pursuit; Double doors begin to open to me and every crooked places are made straight.

18. Every door of opportunity closed against me before now, start to open and every lost opportunity begin to reopen

with double blessings. Job, promotions, ministry, marriage, immigration, scholarships, business, fruitfulness etc.

19. I pray that my church, ministry or local assembly be granted a door of utterance to declare the gospel with all boldness and the mysteries of Christ be revealed to all men.

20. I gain access through the keys of prayer into a realm of uncommon insight and divine revelation in the word of God. The eyes of my understanding are flooded with light from today.

21. I am a solution carrier, the salt of the earth, the light of the world! I fulfill my destiny in Christ Jesus and my spirit man is quickened and ablaze by the fire of the word. I am strengthened to run my race and finish well in Jesus' name.

Give thanks for answered prayers!

## DELIVERANCE FROM STRANGE BATTLES:
(Fight My Battles, O Lord!!)

1. Thank You Father for the gift of life and the power of salvation at work in me.

2. Thank You for the blood of everlasting covenant that speaks victory in my life at all times. Thank You for complete forgiveness of my sins.

3. Thank You Lord for being my defender and shield from all the battles of life. Thank You for winning seen and unseen battles on my behalf.

4. Thank You Lord for placing me in the seat of Christ over all principalities and powers and rulers of darkness!

5. Father Lord, release supernatural baptism of understanding

and let the knowledge of Christ's victory flood my mind and innermost being. Strengthen me for battle and equip me for spiritual warfare! Teach my fingers to fight and train my hands for war.

6. Lion of Judah! Locate the strongman troubling my life and cut him off like Goliath so that all the smaller strongmen would fade away; help me to locate the ring-leader and make him a scapegoat so that the others will flee from before me.

> **1 Samuel 17:51**- *Therefore David ran and stood over the Philistine, took his sword and drew it out of its sheath and killed him, and cut off his head with it. And when the Philistines saw that their champion was dead, they fled.*

7. Send me help O Lord, like the You sent people to help David in 1 Chronicles 12:22 send me a great host, like the host of God to fight every strange battle arrayed against me and my family.

8. Father, through Your instruction make me an expert in war, with all the instruments of war. I refuse to give in to fear or be of a double heart. Let my household be delivered from every dark battle through the knowledge of Your word.

9. As I wait upon the Lord I am renewed in strength like an eagle and I will not faint or fall where others failed in Jesus' name. My spiritual walk gets better and my race in life gets swifter for God's glory. I gain supernatural speed for lost time and recover every lost opportunity in Jesus' name.

10. Father Lord! Contend with my contenders and let them be satisfied with their own flesh who wants to eat my flesh! Let those who want to drink my blood become drunk with their own blood in Jesus' name!

11. Lord, fight my battles in the dream and every battle in my sleep. Disgrace every attacker of my destiny and destroy every troubler of my peace! Silence every Haman the Agagite attacking my lifting in Jesus' name.

12. Mighty Man of War, go into my past and defeat every generational battles arrayed against me. Step into my present and my future to silence every battle in my life.

13. Lion of Judah destroy every work of Amalek operating in my family, work and finances. Let the blood of Jesus speak against every lawful captivity in my bloodline.

14. From today, I refuse to turn back from adversity and will not fail in the day of adversity. The Holy Spirit arms me with the strength and might required to address every battle that comes my way in the name of Jesus.

15. I decree that I will not take the bait or fall into the snare of the enemy in Jesus' name. I fulfill all obedience by Christ Jesus and every disobedience is avenged on my health, marriage, career, ministry and destiny in Jesus' name.

16. No weapon fashioned against me shall prosper and every tongue that reports me in the council of the wicked is disgraced and condemned in Jesus mighty name. Every evil gathering where my name is mentioned; scatter by fire!

17. Captain of the Host, release Your fearful beasts and militant angels to fight with all the unrepentant enemies from my father's house, mother's house and in-laws house.

18. I rejoice today because my warfare is accomplished through Christ Jesus and I am more than a conqueror in all battles of life! I refuse to die like men or fall like one of the princes!

19. As I match forward as a soldier of Christ, I return to sender every evil arrow or the evil one and nullify every retaliation arrow fired against me as an intercessor by the blood of the Lamb.

20. Mighty Man of war, go ahead of me and make every crooked path straight, level out every mountain and elevate every valley. Empower my feet to climb the highest mountain with wisdom and let me emerge at the top at all times.

21. Anoint me as Your battle-axe and Your weapon of war! Make me and my children after me arrows in Your mighty hands. Use us to humiliate the kingdom of darkness in Jesus' name.

Give thanks for answered prayers!


## DELIVERANCE FROM SATANIC TOILING
(I Work And Will Not Labor!)

1. Thank You Lord for the gift of life!

2. Thank You Father for the discovery of divine secrets.

3. Thank You Lord for the blood of Jesus that speaks better things than the blood of Abel on my life.

4. Thank You for the complete forgiveness I have through the blood of everlasting covenant.

5. Thank You for the propitiation of all my sins and shame past, present and future including the sins of my ancestors.

6. Heavenly Father, I bare my chest of any outstanding bill of conscience by the washing of the blood of Jesus.

7. I plead the blood over every work of my hands, my calling and destiny. Jesus paid for my sweat with his sweat, I will no longer sweat for increase in Jesus' name.

8. Heal my head, my hands and my feet; anoint my head for greatness, my hands for exploits and my feet by Your leading alone in Jesus' name.

9. I will no longer labor under the curse of sweating and toiling in Jesus' name. From today I begin to work profitably and enjoy the work of my hands!

10. I refuse to labor for another to enjoy and I will not build for another to inhabit in Jesus' name. I prosper exceedingly in my work and assignment.

11. I was created by God for work and not for labor and toiling so I find profitable work and my life attract and retain increase.

12. I break every collective captivity of failure or poverty. I destroy every power of the Midianites and the terror of wasters in Jesus' name.

13. Jesus wore the crown of thorns so from today I enforce the lifting of my head and clarity of God's vision for my life. I search out the secret of success from the word and cast off every yoke of labor (Matthew 11:28)!

14. My head is healed and anointed to think inventive thoughts and creative inventions that leads to profit. I succeed with the anointing of ease in Jesus' name.

16. I will find profitable work and my feet is ordered by uncommon favor as I become an employer of workers in Jesus' name.
17. I am empowered to bring expansion to every job or business

or ministry where I work and my company will recognize me for it.

18. I will ride upon the high places of the earth in the name of Jesus and I raise others along with me by the blood of Jesus.

19. Like Joseph and Daniel, kings and household names will seek for my partnership in business and ventures in the name of Jesus.

20. I operate by the higher intelligence of God to run projects, ventures and businesses like Adam before the fall.

21. Lord preserve that which keeps You excited about my destiny with Your everlasting arm. I will keep going forward and upward.

22. Grant me access to the company of kings and nobles. Let me dine with royalty and let me be favored by greatness.

23. Let double doors of opportunity open for me and let my gate of success be opened continually. Open my eyes to recognize uncommon opportunities.

24. Father, by Your favor cause me to walk on high places of the earth and let my feet be ushered into palaces and quarters of kings.

25. This year, I must eat the good of the land and I must eat honey from the flinty rock (hard places). The rock will pour for me rivers of oil.

26. Father Lord, let scarcity become plenty in Jesus' name. Let my feet be washed with butter and my hands with empowered for exploits.

27. Father, I receive a fresh oil of distinction and uncommon lifting above my peers and experts in my field. I enforce the finished work of Christ concerning my work.

28. According to the word of the Lord, I will do the work that I enjoy and enjoy the profit of my work. I am blessed and also a channel of blessing.

29. I declare that I am blessed exceedingly and the Lord will make my name great as He promised my father Abraham.

30. I move forward with speed, I go upward until I become very great and every seed I have sown in the kingdom returns to me a hundredfold in Jesus' name.

## DELIVERANCE FROM SATANIC YOKES
(I am Blessed and cannot be Cursed!)

1. Thank You Jesus for dying for me on the cross of Calvary and writing my name in the Book of Life. Thank You Heavenly Father for Your love that never fails over me and my generation after me.

2. Thank You Lord for translating from the kingdom of darkness to the kingdom of Your marvelous light. Thank You for washing me clean from every generational sins and evil covenants by the blood of Jesus!

3. Thank You for the new covenant that produces life giving blessings for me and my offspring.

4. Father! Go to my foundation and visit every error with the blood of Jesus. Forgive my family of every sin of idolatry. Like Gideon and Elijah I chose to build an altar for Your name! I destroy and throw down every evil altar in Jesus' name.

4. I cancel every dark covenant in my generation by the Abrahamic covenant I have in Christ Jesus. Let the blood of Jesus purge my foundation of idolatry to the 3rd and 4th generation backwards. I will no longer pay for the sins of my forefathers and my children will not carry any evil consequences in Jesus' name.

5. Father! Show my adversary that You are my Defender! Silence the mouth of the accuser on my behalf! Problems that repeat themselves through the bloodline I cancel you by the blood of Jesus.

6. From today, every trend of household wickedness operating in my life be terminated in Jesus' name.

7. Every handwriting of ordinances against my ancestry be blotted out by the blood of Jesus.

8. Every genetic disorder or compromised blood in my family tree be healed in Jesus' name. Generational sicknesses and disorder be dismantled by fire in Jesus' name. I defy every covenant of calamity and trends of untimely death over myself, my husband and children.

9. My family tree will no longer bear seeds of sickness, failure or sorrow in Jesus' name. I break every evil trend of genetic sicknesses and generational disorders by the blood of Jesus. I denounce every genetic affliction passed down through my bloodline. I render the effects null and void over myself and my children.

10. I defy every generational flaws and traps in Jesus' name. It will not affect me or my children. The trend that skips generation to arrest a victim will not touch me or my family! Foundational poverty covenant break in Jesus' name. Yoke of barrenness be broken and profitless labor be destroyed.

11. I break every trend of marital failure or evil delays in Jesus' name. I destroy the yoke of divorce and refuse to inherit widowhood in Jesus' name. I intercede for my parents and siblings that from today they will no longer carry the trend of evil covenants.

12. Every good thing that has been stolen from my forefathers I receive a thousand gold restoration in Jesus' name. A good man leaves an inheritance for His children's children, so I leave only blessings for my generation after me in Jesus' name.

13. The Lord will make my family a household name like the house of David and His Son Jesus Christ. I enforce the covenant of life over any covenant of death in my fathers house, mothers house or in-laws house. I refuse to carry a vagabond spirit because of the wickedness of my forefathers. I break such covenants by the blood of Jesus (Psalms 109).

14. Every evil covenant made as a result of my birth must be broken by the blood of Jesus. Every evil exchange made at my wedding be destroyed in Jesus' name. Combination forces from my father's house, my mother's house and my in laws' house catch fire in Jesus' name!

15. Every household wickedness fighting my progress in life receive the fire of God's judgment. Any evil collaboration against my family be scattered by fire. My children and my generation after me will serve The Lord with fervency.

16. Let God arise from the place of thunder and rain hailstorm on all evil perpetrators in my bloodline. I will rise! My children shall rise and my generations after me. I will not be limited by the vagabond spirit!

17. Father, use me to rewrite my family history like Jabez - change my name from sorrow to honor! I release myself

and my household from every collective and lawful captivity through the blood of Jesus.

18. I exercise authority over every household serpent and scorpion be crushed under my feet in Jesus' name. You ancestral monitor of failure be consumed by the Consuming fire of God. There shall be no divination against me or enchantment against my family.

19. I silence every tongue that rises against me in judgment be disgraced and condemned in Jesus' name. I am set free to conquer where my parents have failed because I am more than a conqueror through Him who loved me. I am elevated beyond every limitation that stopped my predecessors in my father and mother's house.

20. I denounce every failure at the edge of success plaguing my bloodline in Jesus' name. I will succeed where others failed, I will live longer where others died and I will be fruitful in every area of my life in Jesus' name.

21. My teeth will not be put on edge because of the sour grapes that my father's hate in Jesus. My children's teeth will not be put on edge because of the sins of my fathers.

Give thanks for answered prayers!


## DELIVERANCE FROM SATANIC DELAY
(Remember me, O Lord!)

1. Thank Father, for writing my name in the Lamb's book of life.

2. Thank You Lord for keeping a book of remembrance in heaven for those who serve You.

3. Thank You for the blood of Jesus that pleads on my behalf for remission and redemption.

4. Thank You for keeping this appointment with me in life and destiny.

5. Thank You Father because today is my day of remembrance! My time has come.

6. Thank You for turning my story for Your glory and my shame for Your fame!

7. Father Lord, visit my foundation today and correct every error holding me down in Jesus' name.

8. Let all the attackers of my progress receive the reward of Haman the Agagite! Let everyone plotting my downfall gather to celebrate my lifting in Jesus' name.

9. Father, help me to succeed where others have failed. Single me out by Your favor today, visit my case for good!

10. Father, open the book of remembrance for me today so that all those who looked down on me will begin to look up to me.

11. Lord let me shine as Your precious jewel; let the whole world know that I serve a living God. Decorate my life for Your glory!

12. Jesus my great high priest, I call on You to invoke on my behalf the mystery of remembrance in the order of Malachi 3:16-18!

13. I will shine, prosper and flourish no matter the opposition against me in the name of Jesus. I will go forward and upward

till I become very great!

14. From today, I will no longer be despised, pitied or ignored in life from this moment I shall be envied like the Philistines envied Isaac.

15. Lord, reveal to me what You have called me to be and do in this life, in  this season and in my present location by Your Holy Spirit.

16. Father, help me to redeem all the lost time, glory and results. Let Your promises concerning me find speedy fulfillment in Jesus' name!

17. Father Lord, move me to the center of Your will for my life . Move me from the dunghill and set me among princes in Jesus' name.

18. Remove every supplanter of my destiny by thunder. Dethrone every impersonator taking my position on the throne by fire.

19. You have called me to a life of glory and virtue; everything that brings shame and disgrace must vanish today by the blood of the Lamb of glory.

20. My glory arise! My star begin to shine - you have hidden in obscurity enough. My destiny, receive the anointing to shine as a star in life by Christ Jesus.

21. Every cord of failure break! Every chain of stagnation be destroyed. Every yoke of limitation catch fire in Jesus' name.

22. Every stumbling block on my path receive the touch of God and become stepping stones. Every obstacle in my way turn into miracles in Jesus' name.

23. I reject the trend of bitterness in my foundation and decree a better quality of life for me and my household in Jesus' name.

24. Father, let my name come up on the lips of kings and let me become relevant in king's palaces like Daniel. Anointing of diligence begin to speak for me!

**If you desire children pray for your self but if your quiver is full, intercede for others. Song - Remember me O Lord.

25. Father, open all the wombs that have been shut down by household wickedness and evil covenants.

26. Let all those believing God for children receive their miracle babies like Hannah and Sarah according to the time of life (9 months)

27. Heal every broken parts of their body and replace every missing part with new organs. Make abundant supply what is not enough in both men and women.

28. Any evil altar tying down any womb or destiny receive the judgment fire of God! Open great doors of testimonies and shock my enemies with Your presence!

29. My head receive turn around for greatness and become what God ordained you to be (Anoint your head with oil).

30. Father, touch my head and shatter every veil of darkness covering my glory!

31. Father Lord shatter every evil covenant holding back my breakthrough in the womb. Deliver me from every placental covenant.

32. My womb, hear the word of the Lord. Be fruitful, multiply

and replenish. Function as a carrier of life and a bearer of greatness!

33. Father Lord, remember me like Hannah and cause me to laugh like Sarah. Today remember me for fruitfulness and unlimited breakthroughs.

34. Let all my mockers gather to celebrate my victory. Let me sing a new song like Elizabeth and Hannah!

NOTE: Look around you for anything or document that represent what you need breakthrough for: immigration papers, check books, resumes, diplomas or certificates, medical reports, wallets etc.

35. Remember me o Lord! Visit my case with uncommon favor. Let me find grace in Your sight like Noah. Rise up to defend me like Hezekiah. Turn my story around like Esther. Give me a 24 hours miracle concerning this matter (*Mention it*).

36. Remember me O Lord! Visit me with a miracle that no man can give nor any government offer to me.

37. Remember our land, O Lord, to heal it (*mention your country, city or neighborhood*).

38. Remember my father's house and my mother's house for mercy. Bless my sibling and our entire generation

39. Remember Your covenant of blessing to me and my generation after me to the 3rd and 4th generation

40. Every stolen benefit belonging to my forefathers I collect in full today with interest by the blood of Jesus!

Give thanks for answered prayers!

# DELIVERANCE FROM DEMONIC AFFLICTION
(Heal Me O Lord!)

1. Thank You Lord for the power of redemption at work in my life.

2. Thank You for the resurrection power that raised Jesus from the dead working in my body to quicken me.

3. Thank You Father for accepting me into the beloved by the blood of Jesus

4. Thank You for wiping away all my sins by the blood of Jesus and every legal accusation against me annulled by the death of Your son Jesus.

5. Thank You Jesus for blotting out the handwriting of ordinances against me by Your precious blood and erasing all that was contrary to my lifting. Thank You for giving me a clean slate and a brand new life

6. Father, cleanse me and sanctify me inside out with the power of Your word. Let You healing virtue flow through me

7. Son of David have mercy on me! Have mercy on my family! Have mercy on my ancestry! Have mercy on my children and my generation after me!

8. I receive complete freedom from all the curse of the law that may have worked against me in the past

9. Heal me O Lord and I will be healed! Save me and I will be saved! Heal every area of my life

10. I speak strength to my heart in Jesus' name. Pump blood in the right amount, arteries and valves open up to infuse life.

11. Kidney function properly in Jesus' name remove all the waste from my blood and digestive system.

12. Liver resume normal function right now and regulate all chemical balance in my body. Remove all the waste and poison in my blood in Jesus' name.

13. My lungs receive the breathe of God and supply oxygen to vital parts of my body for energy. Remove every carbon-dioxide resulting in exhaustion.

14. My brain receive divine anointing in Jesus' name to think fast, stay calm and regulate my nervous system. I refuse to be afflicted mentally because Jesus paid the price for me.

15. My knees and legs receive strength, my hands become empowered and my finger and toes be swift to perform God's purpose in Jesus' name.

16. I break every yoke of demonic afflictions and arrows of sickness by the blood of Jesus. Every arrow of enchantment and divination return to sender!

17. My stomach and digestive tract become satisfied with the goodness of the Lord. Even when I eat poison it will no longer harm me. I speak order to every disorder in Jesus' name.

18. Every habitation of evil in my body causing me pain or sorrow receive the judgment fire of God right now in Jesus' name.

19. Every abnormal swelling, growth or inflammation be consumed by the consuming fire of God. I subject the names to the name of Jesus (*mention the name the doctors called it*).

20. I receive the health and strength that the word of God

gives. I exchange human life with the divine life of Jesus right now.

21. I refuse every generational diseases passed down from my father's house, my mother's house and my in-laws house over me and my generation after me in Jesus' name.

22. I choose to believe the report of the Lord for my health. I am healed, I am free, I live long and I lay hands on the sick and they recover in Jesus' name.

23. I and my household are completely free from the perilous pestilence and contagious diseases out there including seasonal flu! They have no power over us in Jesus' name.

24. I bind every strongman that are enforcing sickness and diseases in my bloodline. I defeat every household wickedness by the blood of Jesus.

25. I confess total victory over psychological and mental affliction. I bind every spirit of confusion or anxiety. I free myself from any emotional bondage in Jesus' name.

26. I declare normal function to the part of my brain and soul that controls sleep. I will enjoy sweet sleep and I will not oversleep nor get lethargic.

27. I destroy every evil altar that have been erected against my health. I arrest every evil personality operating there by the fire of the Holy Ghost.

28. I decree blindness on every evil eye that is monitoring my life and family in Jesus' name. I break free from every oppression of the wicked!

29. Sickness pack your load and go! I have a covenant with life

and not death in Jesus Christ. Decay be destroyed, affliction be wasted!

30. I speak wholeness to my spirit, my soul and my body according to the word of God in 3 John 2. I prosper in every area of my existence in Jesus' name.

31. My youth is renewed like the eagles and my vision is sharper as my day progresses. I am satisfied with long life.

32. The hair on my head be fruitful and multiply! My teeth regain your edge and my perception increase by the spirit of the Lord.

33. No evil shall befall me, no calamity shall come near my dwelling. My family enjoy divine covering from all ills in Jesus' name. Terror is far from me!

34. My womb receive fruitfulness, healing and wholeness. My reproductive system be healed and empowered like Abraham and Sarah!

35. I intercede for my family members afflicted with ...(*name them*) I plead the blood of Jesus for their healing in Jesus' name.

36. I intercede for my friends that are sick - Lord touch them with Your healing hands. Let them know joy instead of pain.

37. I intercede for the land (*mention your city, state and nation*). Heal our land O Lord! Let righteousness exalt us. Let salvation become our banner!

38. I intercede for my parents that the sickness that affects people in old age will not touch them. I break every yoke of sickness over them in Jesus' name.

39. I intercede for my church, heal my Church family. Touch us where we hurt the most. Move us to the next level by fire

40. Father, heal my life, my destiny, my career, my ministry, my career, my finances, my academics, my business, my marriage. (*Tell Him whatever needs healing*)!

Give thanks for answered prayers!


## DELIVERANCE FROM MARITAL YOKE
(Marital Breakthrough I)

1. Lord, grant me restoration of all lost years in love and intimacy by the blood of Jesus! Lord, grant us restoration of all lost years together by the blood of Jesus! Grant my spouse and I restoration in all areas career, academics, fruitfulness and dignity.

> **Joel 2:25** - *And I will restore to you the years that the locust hath eaten, the cankerworm, and the caterpiller, and the palmerworm, my great army which I sent among you.*

2. Father! Divinely restore my marital destiny by Christ Jesus! Remove every shame and reproach from my life in Jesus' name. Wipe away my secret tears and destroy every evil trend of delay or divorce in my ancestry.

> **Isaiah 54:4-6** - *Do not fear, for you will not be ashamed;Neither be disgraced, for you will not be put to shame;For you will forget the shame of your youth,And will not remember the reproach of your widowhood anymore. For your Maker is your husband,The Lord of hosts is His name; And your Redeemer is the Holy One of Israel; He is called the God of the whole earth. For the Lord*

*has called you Like a woman forsaken and grieved in spirit, Like a youthful wife when you were refused," Says your God.*

3. I will not lack my mate in Jesus' name. My marriage will not fail and I reject every form of divorce. I declare that I am blissfully married by the blood of the lamb.

> **Isaiah 34:16** - *Search from the book of the Lord, and read: Not one of these shall fail; Not one shall lack her mate. For My mouth has commanded it, and His Spirit has gathered them.*

4. I am free from every curses of the law and my bloodline, I break free from the evil trend in my father's house or my mother's house. I am free from any generational curses affecting my marital destiny. I break free from "like father like son" syndrome or "like mother like daughter" patterns in Jesus' name!

> **Galatians 3:13-14** - *Christ has redeemed us from the curse of the law, having become a curse for us (for it is written, "Cursed is everyone who hangs on a tree"), that the blessing of Abraham might come upon the Gentiles in Christ Jesus, that we might receive the promise of the Spirit through faith.*

5. Grant me the marital joy that brings no sorrow in the name of Jesus. Let all gather to celebrate with me. Father, let my joy be permanent.

> **Proverbs 10:22** - *The blessing of the Lord makes one rich, And He adds no sorrow with it.*

6. Deliver me from all my fears, let me not be ashamed oh Lord!

**Psalm 34:4-5** - *I sought the Lord, and He heard me, And delivered me from all my fears. They looked to Him and were radiant, And their faces were not ashamed.*

7. I break free from every generational yoke and household covenant that works against marriage in my father's house, mother's house and my in-law's house in the mighty name of Jesus!

**Isaiah 52:1-2** - *Awake, awake! Put on your strength, O Zion; Put on your beautiful garments, O Jerusalem, the holy city! For the uncircumcised and the unclean shall no longer come to you. Shake yourself from the dust, arise; Sit down, O Jerusalem! Loose yourself from the bonds of your neck, O captive daughter of Zion!*

8. Because God plants the (Solitary) lonely in families; He will build my family from the foundation. I will not be lonely any more in my own home.

**Psalm 68:5-6** - *Father to the fatherless, defender of widows— this is God, whose dwelling is holy. God places the lonely in families; he sets the prisoners free and gives them joy. But he makes the rebellious live in a sun-scorched land.*

9. Every evil personality or strongman against my marriage be buried alive in Jesus' name! Any forces making my spouse avoid me be shattered by fire.

**Isaiah 49:24-26** - *Who can snatch the plunder of war from the hands of a warrior? Who can demand that a tyrant let his captives go? But the Lord says, "The captives of warriors will be released, and the plunder of tyrants will be retrieved. For I will* *fight those who fight you, and I will save your children. I will feed your enemies with their own flesh. They will be drunk with rivers of their own blood. All the world will know that I, the Lord, am your Savior and your Redeemer, the Mighty One of Israel."*

10. I and my husband will raise children together as the Lord ordains it. Our children will grow in a safe home and terror will be far from them. Our home shall be established in righteousness. We will be far from oppression in the name of Jesus. No weapon formed against us shall prosper.

**Isaiah 54:13-14,17** - *All your children shall be taught by the Lord, And great shall be the peace of your children. In righteousness you shall be established; You shall be far from oppression, for you shall not fear; And from terror, for it shall not come near you. No weapon formed against you shall prosper, And every tongue which rises against you in judgment You shall condemn. This is the heritage of the servants of the Lord, And their righteousness is from Me," Says the Lord.*

11. My God! Fight for me and defend me. I have no other helper! Deliver me from every strange battle of marriage by Your mercy!

**Isaiah 55:3,12** - *Incline your ear, and come to Me. Hear, and your soul shall live; And I will make an everlasting covenant with you—The sure mercies of David. "For you shall go out with joy, And be led out with peace; The mountains and the hills shall break forth into singing before you, And all the trees of the field shall clap their hands.*

12. Helper of the helpless, help me! Father of the fatherless, defend me! Show me the way forward in my marital destiny.

**Isaiah 50:7** - *"For the Lord God will help Me; Therefore I will not be disgraced; Therefore I have set My face like a flint, And I know that I will not be ashamed.*

13. Remember me o Lord! Like You remembered Hannah. Address my case as You addressed Ruth's marital case.

**Ruth 3:18** - *Then she said, "Sit still, my daughter, until you know how the matter will turn out; for the man will not rest until he has concluded the matter this day."*

14. Settle me o Lord! It is my turn to shine! I must not suffer shame in my marital destiny.

**1 Peter 5:10** - *But may the God of all grace, who called us to His eternal glory by Christ Jesus, after you have suffered a while, perfect, establish, strengthen, and settle you.*

15. I give God high praise and I know He will rise up for me to destroy every enemy of my peace.

**2 Chronicles 20:22-23** - *Now when they began to sing and to praise, the Lord set ambushes against the people of Ammon, Moab, and Mount Seir, who had come against Judah; and they were defeated. For the people of Ammon and Moab stood up against the inhabitants of Mount Seir to utterly kill and destroy them. And when they had made an end of the inhabitants of Seir, they helped to destroy one another.*

16. This Year, I will testify for good according to the word of the Lord! All the adversaries of my home will help to destroy one another in Jesus mighty name.

Give thanks for answered prayers.

(Marital Breakthrough II)

1. Every conspiracy against my marital destiny be shattered by the blood of Jesus! Every demonic gathering of evil counselors be destroyed in Jesus' name.

> **Isaiah 8:12-13** - *"Do not say, 'A conspiracy,' Concerning all that this people call a conspiracy, Nor be afraid of their threats, nor be troubled. The Lord of hosts, Him you shall hallow; Let Him be your fear, And let Him be your dread.*

2. My husband's heart safely trusts in me at all times. We will not struggle with counsel of the third party in our marriage in the name of Jesus. I cast out every spirit of disagreement from our matrimonial home.

> **Proverbs 31:11** - *The heart of her husband safely trusts her; So he will have no lack of gain.*

**FOR MEN**: My heart safely trust in my wife at times. We will not struggle with counsel of the third party in our marriage in the name of Jesus. I cast out every spirit of disagreement from our matrimonial home.

3. My husband/wife and I walk in agreement in our vision and purposes. Our vision complements one another and will not clash. We will hear each other out when we talk and be in agreement when we pray.

> **Amos 3:3** - *Can two walk together, unless they are agreed?*

4. Its time for me to enjoy my marriage, our love is renewed and our covenant is deepened in Jesus' name.

**Ezekiel 16:8** - *"When I passed by you again and looked upon you, indeed your time was the time of love; so I spread My wing over you and covered your nakedness. Yes, I swore an oath to you and entered into a covenant with you, and you became Mine," says the Lord God.*

5. I destroy every influence of the third party in my marriage in Jesus' name. My marriage covenant is between God, my husband and I.

**Ecclesiastes 4:9-12** - *Two are better than one,Because they have a good reward for their labor. For if they fall, one will lift up his companion. But woe to him who is alone when he falls,For he has no one to help him up. Again, if two lie down together, they will keep warm;But how can one be warm alone? Though one may be overpowered by another, two can withstand him. And a threefold cord is not quickly broken.*

6. Every evil tongue that rise against us is condemned and I cancel every counsel of Ahitophel and every evil influence. Only the counsel of the Lord shall stand concerning us.

**2 Samuel 16:21,23** - *And Ahithophel said to Absalom, "Go in to your father's concubines, whom he has left to keep the house; and all Israel will hear that you are abhorred by your father. Then the hands of all who are with you will be strong." Now the advice of Ahithophel, which he gave in those days, was as if one had inquired at the oracle of God. So was all the advice of Ahithophel both with David and with Absalom.*

**Proverbs 19:21** - *There are many plans in a man's heart, Nevertheless the Lord's counsel—that will stand.*

7. I prophesy that our relationship gets better and our friendship grows deeper. Our marriage becomes sweeter and our love deepens intimately as the Lord ordains it in marriage.

> **Ezekiel 37:7** - *So I prophesied as I was commanded; and as I prophesied, there was a noise, and suddenly a rattling; and the bones came together, bone to bone.*

> **Genesis 2:23** - *And Adam said: "This is now bone of my bones And flesh of my flesh; She shall be called Woman, Because she was taken out of Man."*

8. My husband loves me as Christ loves the church. He is willing to give his life for me according to God's word in Ephesians 5:25 & 28,

> *Husbands, love your wives, just as Christ also loved the church and gave Himself for her, So husbands ought to love their own wives as their own bodies; he who loves his wife loves himself.*

**FOR MEN**: I love my wife as Christ loves the church. I am willing to give my life for her according to God's word in Ephesians 5:25 & 28,

> *Husbands, love your wives, just as Christ also loved the church and gave Himself for her, So husbands ought to love their own wives as their own bodies; he who loves his wife loves himself.*

9. Father Lord, speak to my husband when he is awake and talk to him when he sleeps. Touch his heart and give him a permanent encounter with you. Make him a priest of our home and a mentor to our children (**MEN:** Say the same for the wife).

**Matthew 1:19-20** - *Then Joseph her husband, being a just man, and not wanting to make her a public example, was minded to put her away secretly. But while he thought about these things, behold, an angel of the Lord appeared to him in a dream, saying, "Joseph, son of David, do not be afraid to take to you Mary your wife, for that which is conceived in her is of the Holy Spirit.*

10. Our home is a tension free zone filled with the peace of God that passes all human understanding. My husband finds peace at home, I find peace and our children enjoy the peace of Christ. Anyone who visits our home will enjoy the peace in Jesus' name.

**Isaiah 32:18** - *My people will dwell in a peaceful habitation, In secure dwellings, and in quiet resting places.*

Give thanks for answered prayers!

## DELIVERANCE FROM STRANGE BATTLES
(War Against Pharaoh!)

1. Father, thank You for saving me and translating me from the kingdom of darkness to the kingdom of light.

2. Thank You for washing me clean by the precious blood of Jesus and writing my name in the Lamb's book of life.

3. Thank You for breaking every dark covenants and every curse of the law through the precious blood of everlasting covenant.

4. Father, break the teeth of Pharaoh holding down my increase and blessings in Jesus' name. Strike my all my enemies upon

the cheekbone!

5. Lord Jesus with the blast of Your nostril, show every adversary that is limiting my progress that You are my Defender!

6. Pharaoh, let my people go! Let my family go! Let my children go! Let me go!

7. I am that I am, stretch out Your mighty hand and strike Pharaoh and his army oppressing my work, marriage, family or ministry (*mention the area of need*).

8. Father, grant me favor – do not let me go empty handed! Plunder the house of Pharaoh for all my stolen goods (my job, admission, scholarship, anointing, lifting, increase, blessings, properties, dignity, my glory and virtue).

9. Every evil personality from my father's house, my mother's house or in-laws house contending with my destiny finish them off completely today. Give their lives in exchange for my life.

10. Every taskmaster afflicting me or adding burdens to hard labor for me visit them with Your fire of judgment.

11. Show the contender of my destiny that You have completely delivered me by Your blood of everlasting covenant.

12. Every pharaoh negotiating my promotion and progress in life is swallowed up in the red sea of the blood of Jesus today.

13. I destroy every yoke of slavery and poverty mentality operating in my life or family line in Jesus' name.

14. I am going far above every limitation of the adversary that has held people down from my family, town, nation or race.

15. I enforce the covenant of new birth over my life and my children after me in the name of Jesus – give us a household name like David.

16. Make me a sign and a wonder to my world. Use me to rewrite my family history and my generation after me.

17. Father, hide me under Your pillar of cloud by day and Your pillar of fire by night. Let me enjoy perfect health in the land of the living.

18. Father, show me Your glory and take me into the land of fulfillment flowing with milk and honey. Turn every bitterness in my life to sweetness in Jesus' name.

19. Use my life as a testimony to disgrace the power and threatening of pharaoh. Let me enjoy water from the rock and manna from heaven in Jesus' name.

20. Grant me access to land that I did not buy, vineyard that I did not plant and cause me to inherit the houses that I did not build by Your favor.

21. Bless me so that I can be a blessing to others and a financial pillar for kingdom expansion.

Thank God for answered prayers!

# DELIVERANCE FROM DREAM BATTLES
(Visit My Dream and Restore My Vision!)

1. Thank You Lord for the gift of salvation and the cleansing blood of Jesus.

2. Thank You for the gift of life and writing my name in the Book of Life. Thank You for establishing me as a royal priesthood and a holy nation unto You.

3. Thank You for giving me the power to tread upon serpent and scorpions and all the powers of darkness even in my dreams.

4. I cover every day, week, month and years written and allotted to me by God according to His book in Psalm 139:14-16 with the precious blood of the Lamb. I will fulfill my divine assignment in Jesus' name.

5. According to Amos 3:7 the Lord does nothing except he shows it first to His servant the prophet; show me thing to come and bring all things to my remembrance. Anoint my prayer life for prophetic exploits.

6. Father, restore my dreams and visit me with heavenly visions. Replace my self-centered vision with kingdom vision, open my spiritual eyes like Elisha and my spiritual ears like Elijah. Anoint my dreams like Joseph and give me the interpretation of dreams like Daniel.

7. By Your Holy Spirit, flood my understanding with divine mysteries and the details of my destiny. By Your grace bring every single vision and dream to fulfillment according to divine timing.

8. Lord of Host fight all my battles in the dream and defeat

every evil personality contending with me. Destroy every soul-tie (spirit husband, spirit wife, night lovers) from my past with living or dead people by the blood of everlasting covenant.

9. Ancient of Days visit my foundation and destroy every evil altar from my father's house, mother's house and in-laws house affecting my vision and dream. Return to sender every arrow shot at me and let every evil yoke be destroyed (labor, heavy burden, load, yoke, fetters of iron or chains of brass).

10. I operate with the spirit of wisdom and revelation in Christ. I have the understanding of times like the sons of Issachar and I am led by the Spirit into the center of God's will armed with the details of my life, nation and generation in Jesus' name.

11. I bind every strongman operating through my dreams and I denounce every covenant made on my behalf while I was sleeping. I neutralize every arrow and nullify every poison used against me in the dream according to Mark 16:18.

12. Restorer of dreams, restore all my stolen dreams and open new doors of opportunity to me. Shatter every shadow covering my glory and grant me access into heavenly visions through the keys of David.

13. I nullify every dream of toiling and labor in Jesus' name. I reverse every power that returns me back to square-one in my dreams. My path is like a shining light, I make speedy progress and I rise to the top in my career, academics, business and ministry.

14. I empty every emptier by the power in the name of Jesus. I recover all lost glory and virtue by Christ Jesus. My destiny will not be wasted in Jesus' name. I nullify every token of diviners and silence the tongue of liars.

15. From today, counsel flows out of my heart like deep waters, I have the seeing eyes and hearing ears and my spirit man is lighted by the Holy Spirit with high intensity. I know things before they happen because I share in God's secrets.

16. I operate with vision and precision from now on, I cast out every spirit of confusion and bind every demonic activity in my dream in Jesus' name. The Spirit of the Almighty gives me understanding and revelation knowledge.

17. According to the word of the Lord, I see visions during the day and I receive instructive dreams at night in Jesus' name.

18. The Spirit of the Lord instructs my reins at night and his billows flow over my soul at all times.

19. I receive a fresh baptism of the Holy Spirit to manifest in the school of the spirit. The words of wisdom, knowledge, prophesy, diversity of tongues and interpretation of tongues for the profiting of the church.

20. I break every yoke of delay and stagnation! My star arise and my destiny begin to shine according to Isaiah 60:1 Arise, shine; for your light has come! And the glory of the Lord is risen upon you.

21. Just like Joseph my dream shall impact generations and just like Daniel my vision shall transcend generations after me. People will come to the saving knowledge of Christ though my testimony.

Give thanks to God for answered prayers!

## DELIVERANCE FROM SATANIC MANIPULATION
(Sin Nature Must Die!)

1. Thank You Lord for the blood of Jesus that washes me clean from every sin in my past, present and future!

2. Thank You for the blood of sprinkling that speaks mercy for me instead of judgment and the permanent remission of my sins.

3. Thank You Father for the great High Priest of my profession, who was tempted in all ways like me but yet without sin speaking continually on my behalf.

4. Thank You for the irreversible work of salvation done once and for all on the cross of Calvary for me.

5. I receive complete forgiveness from all sins and peace that passes all human understanding by the blood of Jesus.

6. I operate with the grace that has dominion over sin from today and I refuse to be subject to the sin nature or the old man.

7. I destroy every mystery of iniquity by the power in the blood of Jesus and operate with a conscience void of offenses before God and man.

8. According to Hebrews 10:22 I draw near with a true heart in full assurance of faith, having my heart sprinkled from an evil conscience and my body washed with pure water in Jesus' name.

9. According to Hebrews 9:14 my conscience receive cleansing

from dead works to serve the living God through the spotless blood of Christ.

10. Lust of the eye, lust of the eyes and pride of life you will not find expression in me in the name of Jesus! I kill the flesh by the power in the blood of Jesus!

11. I exchange every poor self concept for divine concepts and destroy every low self esteem by the power in the blood of Jesus! I display a supernatural complex at all times.

12. I display the boldness of the righteous and I am exalted in all my ways in Jesus' name. I cannot be condemned by the devil or his cohorts nor attacked with self defeat.

13. Everything Uzziah represents in my life must die; I must behold the glory of the Lord today. Anger, sin, pride, lust, covetousness, defeat (*mention what it is*) get out of my way in Jesus' name.

14. My life is quickened by the resurrection power to overcome every tendency to fall or stumble in Jesus' name. I live in the conviction of the Holy Spirit at all times.

15. I refuse to trust the flesh or depend on myself. I choose to trust in the Lord and depend on him completely from today. I acknowledge Him in all my ways!

16. Foolish thoughts, defiling thoughts, profane thoughts, proud thoughts, sinful thoughts you are not permitted in this vessel anymore - give way to grateful thoughts, wise thoughts, cheerful thoughts, lovely thoughts and victorious thoughts in Jesus' name!

17. I cast down every imagination and high thing that exalts itself against the knowledge of God in my life and bring every single thought to the obedience of Christ Jesus.

18. I will not serve you king self, I dethrone you and enthrone the King of Kings and the Lord of Lords. I refuse to be a slave to sin but a slave to righteousness!

19. I act, think, behave, manifest and look like my heavenly Father as I am transformed into His image daily from one level of glory to another in Christ Jesus!

20. I refuse to retaliate evil with evil but I overcome evil with good in Jesus' name. I am a true ambassador of Christ on the earth. I love where others hate. I conquer where others fail!

21. According Colossians 3:9-10 I put off the old man with his deeds, and I establish today that I have put on the new man who is renewed in knowledge according to the image of Christ Jesus.

22. Righteousness exalts a nation therefore exaltation is my portion in every area of my life. My marriage, career, ministry and academics receive the power to flourish in Jesus' name.

24. I have been made free by the Son of God therefore no bondage can touch my life, work or children. Everything I have is blessed in Jesus' name!

25. From today self-exertion must give way to divine enablement in my life. Self consciousness must become God consciousness. I am favored when I come in and favored when I go out.

26. The blessing of righteousness is mine; The blessing of Abraham is mine; I am blessed to be a blessing and my path shines brighter and brighter in Jesus' name. Poverty mentality become abundance mentality! Sickness mentality become a living mentality!

27. I demolish every power holding me back from fulfilling my God-given destiny in Christ Jesus! I become a force to reckon with for His kingdom.

28. I will not fall from grace in Jesus' name and I will not fall short of the grace of God; I will start well and finish strong!

29. I refute every trap in the flesh to make me fall or fail and I decree in the name of Jesus that the grace of the Lord Jesus, the love of God and the sweet fellowship of the Spirit will keep me till I see my LORD face to face!

30. I grow in the word, I become stronger in prayer and I am empowered to share the good news to the pleasing of my Heavenly Father in Jesus' name!

Give thanks for answered prayers!

# About Raeni Bankole

RAENI BANKOLE is a minister of the gospel with a three-fold calling to this generation; she was born and raised in Southern Nigeria as Omolaraeni Odewole in a Christian family of 8 children. She relocated to the United States of America in 2001 to further her education.

In 1997, while studying at the University of Ibadan she heard the first call to be used as a "Repairer of the Breach and a Restorer of the path for men to dwell in" according to Isaiah 58:12. She worked passionately in the campus fellowship at the University of Ibadan and later served as one of the pioneering leaders of the Winners Youth Fellowship of the Living Faith Church (Winners Chapel) till she moved to the United States.

In the United States she has served fervently in several ministries under the Redeemed Christian Church of God for over 12 years in the Chicago-land area till she resumed full-time ministry in 2013. She currently runs a vibrant prayer school in the Chicago-land area teaching the word of God and showing the secrets of deliverance by the knowledge of the truth. Her passion is to help individuals birth their God-given vision and to nurture those destinies to complete fulfillment. Many of her teachings can be found on Soundcloud.com @ Nehemiah Troop. She is married to Adebowale Bankole and together they have two lovely children.

Her apostolic calling as a watchman and a voice unto nations operates through different branches of Empowerment Mission Agency (NPF) a registered non-profit organization in the United States of America with a mission to empower nations through Christ.

**Mission**: Empowering nations through Christ

**Vision**: Birthing visions and nurturing destinies.

**Repairer of the Breach:** She teaches and preaches the word of God bringing many to the saving knowledge of the Lord and restoring many lost destinies to their divine destiny in Christ Jesus. "And they shall build the old waste places: you shall raise up the foundations of many generations; and you shall be called, The repairer of the breach, The restorer of paths to dwell in." (Isaiah 58:12).

**A Watchman:** As a watchman, she runs an intercessory ministry that has a mandate to raise a global army of intercessors unto the kingdom of our Lord Jesus Christ...I have made you a watchman for the house of Israel; therefore you shall hear a word from My mouth and warn them for Me (Ezekiel 33:7).

**A Voice:** She is a voice crying in the wilderness of life to many in this generation with the mandate to evangelize and prepare many for the coming of our Lord Jesus Christ...The voice of one crying in the wilderness, Prepare ye the way of the Lord, make his paths straight." (Matthew 3:3).

If you would like to invite Raeni Bankole as a teacher of the word at your seminar or church group program; please send an email to Nehemiahtroop@gmail.com.

# Nehemiah Troop Prayer Ministry (NTPM)

*...raising an army of intercessors*

The Nehemiah Troop Prayer Ministry also known as "The Upper Room" is a weekly prayer school that has a mandate to raise fire-branded watchmen for the Kingdom of our Lord Jesus Christ. It follows after the vision of Nehemiah in the bible that didn't rest until he had rebuilt the walls of Jerusalem. He didn't do it alone; he had the king and his brethren(Nehemiah 2:1-20). Like Nehemiah, many of us today must be empowered like Joseph, Esther and Daniel to save our Father's house!

The vision of NTPM is to raise an army of intercessors all across the land and send out the clarion call for the prophet of nations to take their place on the prayer watches like Daniel who ushered their nation and generation into divine purpose.

There is a weekly phone conference every Saturday at 7:00 a.m. (CST) via freeconferencing.com: **Dial 530-881-1300 Access Code 328037**.

A live meeting also holds every 3rd Saturday of the month from 10 a.m. – 12 p.m. at the Schaumburg Renaissance Hotel.

For more details please view news and events at
www.empowermentmission.org or
the group page on facebook (Nehemiah Troop).

# Nehemiah Troop Scholarship Fund (NTSF)

*...empowering lives through education*

Nehemiah Troop Scholarship Fund (NTSF) is a branch of the Raeni Bankole ministry that empowers young people in the Diaspora through education. The vision was born out of a need to help international students schooling abroad pay their tuition. As the coordinator, Raeni Bankole experienced first-hand what most international students with limited resources go through in order to stay in school. She came to the United States in 2001 to earn a masters degree but dropped out of the program after two semesters due to extreme financial hardship. It took over ten years to regain the dream of obtaining a masters' degree and the NTSF is a fulfillment of the vision to repair the breach and restore the path for many generations to dwell in.

The average cost of tuition per semester in the United States is $8000 - $10,000 and most international student cannot work outside the campus to support themselves. They usually have to drop out of school and defer the dream of furthering their education. It is extremely difficult to survive outside school because they also do not have employment authorization to make any living. Staying registered in school helps these young international students maintain F-1 status and achieve their academic dream. Please join us as we empower lives one day at a time through the Nehemiah Troop Scholarship Fund.

# We want to hear from you!

Please send your comments about this book using the contact details below:

Phone: 630-936-8868
E-mail: nehemiahtroop@gmail.com
Website: www.empowermentmission.org

Please include your testimony of help received from this book when you write.
Your prayer requests are welcome.

You can order additional copies of this book or any other book by the author online @
www.amazon.com
or
simply send us an email or call us.

**Dewalette Creations**

Are you an author?

Would you like to have your book published?

It would be our delight to review your manuscript in preparation for an outstanding publication.

CONTACT US:

Phone:
(630) 481-6305

Email:
dewalette@gmail.com
info@dewalette.com